Pieces of the Quilt

The Mosaic of An African American Family

ANITA L. WILLS

Credits for Front Cover Page
Design By Bruce A. Baxter
Photos

(Clockwise)
Vivian Martin-Baxter,
Pierre Pennington (courtesy of Perry Pennington),
Charles Wesley and Annie Bonaparte-Baxter (Baxter Family Collection),
Samuel and Maria Louisa Pinn-Ruth (Ruth Family Collection),
Leah Ruth-Martin,
Leah Ruth & Vivian Martin-Baxter (Martin Family Collection),
Charles F. Martin (Martin Family Collection),
Ida E. Ruth-Jones (Jones Family Collection),
(Center> Sgt. Robert A. Pinn (Pinn Family Collection)

ISBN: 1-4392-3585-6
ISBN-13: 9781439235850

Visit www.booksurge.com to order additional copies.

Dedication

This book is dedicated to my children, Bruce, Keith, Kerry, Cynthia; and grandchildren Jayla, Jaylen, Kmani, Kerry Junior, Cache; and my Great-Grand daughter, Azhira. To the memory of my parents, George and Vivian Martin-Baxter, who taught us wisdom and patience. This book is also dedicated to the memory of my ancestors who endured so much, and in facing impossible odds, persevered. Last but not least, to the Highest Creator, who has sustained me and mine.

TABLE OF CONTENTS

ACKNOWLEDGEMENTS

There are clerks, historians, authors, and everyday people, who assisted in this quest. This assistance received has proved invaluable. Following are some of those whose assistance was invaluable. Many of the names are the same ones who assisted with the previous book, Notes And Documents of Free Persons of Color. Thanks and appreciation for the original design of this book cover to, Bruce Baxter. There are numerous people who have been of assistance, especially those who are working in the various repositories.

Thanks go to Cousin Vanessa Julye, who has traveled and filmed many areas where our ancestors lived. A special thanks to Gil Sipkema, a Canadian cousin, who assisted me with the Bruxton Settlement. A special thank you to cousin Louise Nocho, who gave me so much information on that line. He is ailing, but is always in my thoughts and prayers.

Thank you to my grandsons who read my first book, and had a lot of questions about our ancestors. Cousin Louise Hinton and Aunt Cora have shared many pictures and stories with me about our ancestors. Thank you to Cousin Perry, the Jones Family, and family members who shared pictures for the cover of this book.

Although my parents have have passed on, they are with me, in spirit and in my dreams. To all of the ancestors, thank you for allowing me to stand on your shoulders.

5/2/2014
Kristen,
Enjoyed meeting you, please enjoy this book which is a history only possible in America
Coretta L. Nell

PREFACE

Over many years, my mother told us about our family history. Those stories were a comfort to us growing up, in 1950's Coatesville Pennsylvasnia. Once we moved away from Coatesville, our lives changed quite a bit. There was little time for my mother to share, as she struggled to keep our family together. In 1978, when we were living in Oakland California my mother told us about our ancestor, The Reverend Robert Pinn. He was a Baptist Minister in Philadelphia, after the Civil War. It was at that time that my mother and I made a pact to document our family history.

This is the second book written by me the first being, Notes and Documents of Free Persons of Color. This book is a narrative of those in my family who led extraordinary lives, like Elijah Johnson, one of the founders of Monrovia Liberia. This book is written in narrative form, and is an easier read. From Pennsylvania through Virginia, into Liberia and beyond. There is also information on relatives who emigrated to Canada. Most of this information was supplied by cousin Gil Sipkema, a descendant of William Parker. He is one of our Canadian relatives, and a historian. Another cousin whose ancestors settled in Canda is Margaret Green-Givens, a Lewis descendant. There is also a chapter on DNA that contains information for those who may be on the fence about testing.

Within the pages there is something for everyone, whether beginners, or experienced family historians. It has a wonderful story line, for those who want a good story.

Thank you to everyone who gave me the "UMP," I needed to complete this work.

⌘ ⌘ ⌘

CHAPTER ONE

⁄ ⁄

IT SEEMS LIKE YESTERDAY

It seems like yesterday, when our family lived at 657 South First Avenue, in South Coatesville Pennsylvania. We called it "The Avenue," so it would not sound too rural and country. After all, we were contending with Philadelphia, the big city to the south of us. Philly was hip and urban, and we were a small rural community, in the middle of Chester County. There may have been five thousand people in South Coatesville when I was growing up. That is if you considered White Hill, and other parts of the greater community. The Avenue was a predominantly African American Community (or Colored as we were called) consisting of about five blocks.

Seven children were born to my parents, George and Vivian Baxter after their marriage in 1941. My oldest brother, George Junior, was born in December of 1941 and the youngest Kimberly was born in 1957. We were stair step children, with about two years between each. The other siblings in the household were Ronald, Nathan, Anthony, Anita (me), and Carolyn. South Coatesville was our home, and where I spent the first twelve years of my life.

Small businesses, mostly African American, dotted the Avenue there was; Jacks' Grocery Store, The Bongo club, Wesley's Barber Shop, Jimmie Lee's Store, Hatfield's Cleaners, Becks' Hairdresser, and Prince Hudson's Hat and Tie Shop. One of the favorite hangouts was the Italian sandwich shop, owned by Nicky and Lena DeMateo, an Italian Family. They also owned a Beer Garden, which was a hot spot on the weekends. We had our own Police Chief, Beverly Burton and my father was the town Constable, and was also our local Exterminator.

THE BOROUGH OF COATESVILLE

The Borough of Coatesville was incorporated by the Court of Quarter Sessions of Chester County in 1867. It was taken wholly from Valley Township, and is situated in the Great Valley, where it is crossed by the west branch of Brandywine, and embraces territory on both sides of that stream. A village long known as Midway, situated on the Pennsylvania Railroad west of the Brandywine, was included within its boundaries, and is now generally known in common parlance as West Coatesville. The Village of Midway was just half-way between Philadelphia and Columbia, the original terminal of the railroad, and hence its name.

Coatesville was named in honor of the Coates family, settlers from Ireland. Moses Coates, the ancestor of the family, with his wife Susanna, came from Ireland about 1717, and settled in Charlestown Township, Chester County, whence some of their children removed to East Caln. William Fleming was a settler near Coatesville. His wife Mary was a sister of John and Thomas Moore, who settled at Downingtown. The Fleming family are now quite numerous. At an early period they owned a considerable quantity of land in the Great Valley, on both sides of the west branch of Brandywine.

In the 1950's, Chester County was constructing subdivisions for the Eastern Europeans who were pouring in. The Newspapers advertised housing, and even rooms stating, "No Colored need apply." The papers also advertised jobs that stated, "No Colored need apply." That was the face of our conservative community in the 1950's, one that gave with one hand, and took away with the other. Yet many blacks fled the south to Pennsylvania seeking more opportunities and wanting a better life.

During the 1950's our community was in an economic boom, fueled by Lukens' Steel Mill and the Cold War. We were in a Cold

War with Russia, and not too long out of World War II. Joseph McCarthy held sway with the United States Senate, as they ushered in the McCarthy Era. Anyone accused of being a Communist Sympathizer could be dragged in front of Congress and questioned. The accusation of being a Communist Sympathizer destroyed many lives, whether or not there was truth to the charges.

Lukens' Steel Mill was a major manufacturer of Steel used to build Missiles, Airplanes, and in Ship Building. In the hills of Pennsylvania, Iron ore and coal were being mined and sent to Bethlehem and Lukens' Steel Mill to be processed. The second largest employer in the region was the Veteran's Hospital, where injured soldiers were sent for treatment.

The African Americans who worked in the Steel Mill were laborers, and received less pay, than their white counterparts. Pennsylvania was just a little more progressive than its' southern neighbors. The racism that existed was subtle, only to those who did not recognize it. For instance, we were not allowed to play at Ash Playground, nor swim in the swimming pool with white children. Few white children attended Hustonville Elementary School which was a stones through away from, White Hill. Our parents, who were required to pay taxes, had far less benefits than the whites. When we went to the Silver Theater to see movies, the section designated for coloreds was in the Balcony. We (coloreds) were not allowed to stay at the Coatesville YWCA downtown, nor at the Coach and Four Inn, a fancy Hotel on Main Street. The other place few of us ventured into was the Coatesville Hospital.

Yet it was a safe haven for the daughter of Strom Thurmond, Essie Mae Washington. She lived in Spruces about a mile away from South First Avenue. My mother did not mention Essie Mae Washington, by name even though they were the same age. She did mention that there were people in our community of mixed raced background from the South. This included her Grandfather, Samuel Ruth, the son of a slave woman and the white man who owned her. She told of him coming north with the 54th Massachusetts, as a Water Boy and that he thought his brother Daniel had been killed by the White Militia. It turns out that Daniel Ruth was very much alive and living in Savannah Georgia after the Civil War.

The light-skinned children who were sent north, were informally adopted. They lived with families who may or may not have been related. There was a network which reached from the south into Pennsylvania, not unlike the Underground Railroad. Many of these children were the offspring of powerful white southerner men, like Strom Thurmond. Their indiscretions were put on anything smoking (bus, train, car), and headed north.

A HISTORY LESSON

There is always the back-story, things that happen that children do not know about, and would not understand. In those days, you would be hard pressed to find anyone who veered from, "Spare the Rod, and Spoil the Child." The schools administered Corporal Punishment, in the form of a paddle on the backside, or a ruler on the knuckles. The former has not been administered to me, but the latter has one time, and boy did it sting.

There was an incident at Hustonville Elementary School, in which our parents confronted the Principal Ms. Redmond. The teachers and Principal at Hustonville Elementary School were white females; except for our Uncle Isaac, the Janitor. Almost ninety percent of the students were African American and the rest were white. We sometimes went to the school on Saturday's to learn songs, take piano lessons, or practice for plays. The Principal, Ms. Redmond was teaching some students to sing, Old Black Joe. The song is supposedly a Negro Spiritual, but Negroes were not singing it. It was a song, which was written after the Civil War and an insult to blacks.

When the black parents found out the children were asked to sing that song, they descended on Ms. Redmond's office. I am told it was quite a scene up there, with the irate parents (including my own), reading her the riot act. Old Black Joe was taken off the song list, and any other songs the parents did not approve of. Another incident that stands out is when my brother Anthony was paddled by Ms. Redmond, and Granny Baxter heard about it.

On hearing about the incident she got out of her rocking chair and headed up the hill to the School. There were few occasions where Granny got out of her rocking chair, during the day. She even ate her meals in that chair which looked like it was a hundred years old. Granny hoisted her large frame up that hill to the school, and told Ms. Redmond, "Don't you ever put your hands on any of my grand children." All of the rage built up from living in the segregated south, and the humiliation of two hundred years of slavery, was taken out . Granny was about five feet four inches tall, a large brown-skinned woman. Ms. Redmond knew and respected Granny, which is probably why she apologized to her that day. That was the last time granny climbed the hill to Hustonville Elementary School. Ms. Redmond was one of those who attended my Grandmother's funeral in 1971.

THOSE WERE THE DAYS

During summer months, we had activities at Hustonville Elementary School, such as baseball, and games to keep us busy. The older children sometimes came there to hang out, but they seldom bothered us. My favorite activity was climbing trees especially the large apple tree on the playground. I climbed to the top of the tree, put my legs around the branch, and hung upside down, studying the ground below. My plaits pointed towards the ground below, as did my arms, as I swung back and forth on the branch. The birds and Squirrels in the tree studied me, and I studied them. Whenever we went out to play my mother would tell us not to eat those Green Apples. The one time I did eat one, my stomach cramped up, and it was not a pleasant experience.

Those were the, "Good Old Days," as we practiced and took direction from our Coach Ransom. He was light-skinned with freckles and always smiling. My position was usually first base, or outfield, but getting up to bat was the best part. Mr. Ransom was our Playground Director in the summer, and some of the parents volunteered with other activities. At the end of summer, the community got together, and had festivities, including Horseshoes, and Sack Races. By September, we headed back to school, and our teachers.

As our Family Historian, my mother knew the backgrounds of almost everyone in the community. This was especially true of the principal and teachers at Hustonville Elementary School, who were all white. Ms. Laird was, "Funny," and lived alone on White Hill, with only her dog for company. Ms. Redmond was married (although we called her Ms.), and her people came from North Carolina. Ms. Berkeheiser lived by herself in her parent's house on White Hill, and went to High School with my father. Ms. Hatfield was not married, did not date, and had no children. She lived alone on White Hill in the house where she grew up.

HOME IS WHERE THE HEART IS...,

Although we were not supposed to be listening to secular music, it was hard to ignore especially when Dick Clark's American Band Stand show, came on. One of us would stand by the door, and another would look out the window. If mom or dad was headed up the alley, a warning went out, and we turned the Television to Howdy Doody, or the Life of Riley. My brother Ronald had a 45-rpm Record Player, and a stack of records.

We watched shows like, "I Love Lucy," "The Life of Riley," and Amos & Andy (until they were canceled). The reception on the Television was depended on the weather, and when the antenna needed adjusting, dad headed for the roof. We watched Television with our parents the night Frankie Lymon was on The Ed Sullivan Show singing, "Why Do Fools Fall in Love." They were also there, when Little Anthony and the Imperials sang, "Tears on my Pillow." We watched the Nat King Cole Show, and Amos & Andy, as a family. I remember waking up one night and my dad and older brothers were watching a cowboy show, a first for me. Friday nights were, "Fight Nights," and the females retreated to the kitchen.

Once a year we got a treat when Paul Robeson performed on Television, complete with black Angels. At the time, we (the children), did not know that our father, was being investigated as a Communist Sympathizer. Paul Robeson was a black actor and activist for the rights of workers, and a so-called Communist Sympathizer. It would be years before the family shared with us the extent of the investigation against dad. My father never spoke of the investigation; it was my mother who came clean, when we were in California. The incident between dad and the FBI is detailed in, Notes and Documents of Free Persons of Color.[1]

As a Constable, my father was busy on the weekends (and paydays), serving warrants on those who went overboard with drinking and fighting. There were bar fights, guns drawn, and tragic deaths during this period, usually from people who had too much to drink. Those arrested were taken to the lockup, to go before an Alderman, and released or bound over. The crimes were by and large from too much drinking, and fighting or other public disturbances. There were no liquor stores, or bars on White Hill, a middle class neighborhood visible from our front porch.

Besides being a Steel Worker and Constable, my father had other ways to bring in money. He was the first African American Exterminator in our community. He mixed his own concoctions, and had many loyal customers. We were pleased when he took care of the roach infestation in our house, which was a converted bakery. The business was pretty good, but his main source of income was working at Luken's Steel Mill. When he took ill he was unceremoniously fired after working there for twenty-four years.

Our family included a large, extended family, those who were adopted in, or play cousins. The church we attended was the Church of God In Christ (COGIC), on South First Avenue. Uncle Alonzo Baxter, was the Pastor of the Church and most of those who attended were Aunts, Uncles, and Cousins. My belief is that the rift between our families was connected to the churches. That is a topic that would require another book to explain. Surfice it to say, those days, attending church was a chance to see my cousins and catch up on some play.

THE HEART OF OUR HOUSE

Our family ate a combination of foods, including Dutch/ German, Soul Food, and Native American. The Dutch recipes always seemed to contain Potatoes, gravy and baked or boiled meats. Soul Food was usually fried chicken, or pork, with some combination of, rice, potato salad, greens, and sweet potatoes. The native foods we ate were typically hominy, pone cakes made from corn, the three sisters, corn, beans and squash, lots of wild berries, and cranberry sauce. I have seen every kind of Squash on my mothers table, including Spaghetti Squash.

The upside of being with my mother was hearing the stories of our ancestors, as she taught me how to bake and cook. Back then, the kitchen was the heart of our house, where everything important took place. Our front door opened into the kitchen, and it was the cleanest room in the house. At night after dinner it was cleaned up, the lights were turned off, and we went into the living room.

During the day, family and friends dropped by, and visited with mom, for coffee and conversation. This was brought to my attention once my mother and I started documenting the family history. She said that black people did not want to talk about history, as it was too painful. The history we learned from my mother was not widely spoken of in our community. There were certain things that were only discussed in private, between family members. My light-skinned mother was talking about all of our ancestors, including those who were white and native.

Mom was light skinned, and compared to Dorothy Dandridge; while dad was, dark skinned and looked like Nat King Cole. The marriage of my parents caused a deep rift between the two families. My Martin Grandparents stated that their seventeen year old daughter (Vivian), was too young to marry, and they should wait. Their issue was the age of their daughter, and not having a dark skinned son. Most of my mother's sisters, who were light-skinnned, married dark skinned men.

The Baxter's did not approve the marriage either, since dad was helping with his younger siblings. My mother believed that Grandmother Baxter did not like her because she was too light. On the Baxter side of our family, the marriages were based on whether the person was a Christian. Some of the friction within the Baxter family had more to do with sibling rivalry, than the light skin, dark –skin issue. When I asked my mother why she married dad, she said that she wanted to make sure that her husband "Was not related." Whatever the argument against their marriage was, they settled it by eloping to Elkton Maryland.

THE HAT CLUB

My mother and the ladies in our family formed a Hat Club, which met several times a month at our house. It was there that they would plot and plan, and shoo us out of the room, because adults were talking. It was also their hat club, with mom as the chief designer. Several of the Aunts showed up at church and someone else was wearing identical hats, on the same day! Seeing an opportunity, mom sat up her own little shop in the kitchen, and was in business.

One day, Aunt Ester Baxter came to our house, upset because another church member wore a hat like hers. Aunt Ester was very light skinned, with reddish brown hair, and Betty Davis Eyes. She was one of those women in the community who took no stuff from anyone. She worked at Embreville State Hospital, and when the same day she quit, demanded, and got her paycheck. She was married to Uncle Sam Baxter, who was soft spoken and quiet, especially when Aunt Ester was there.

Mom ordered Millinery materials, and created a unique hat for Aunt Ester to wear. The next week someone else was there, and she worked on another unique hat design. Mom also knitted and crocheted to order for the women, and they paid her well for it. Most of the sister-in-laws worked and had their own money; something they told mom she needed to do. No matter how much money she had, mom would buy us something, or buy something for the house.

AN END TO THE WONDER YEARS

Living in Coatesville for the first twelve years of my life was the Wonder Years. That is life seemed so simple, and everything went well within our community and family. The community was prospering and the outside world had no real impact, or so it seemed. We got through the dramas of life, and the community gave us (the children) a sense of security. That is the way it should be with children, free to explore and take in the world little by little. That part of my life ended when I was twelve years old, and we moved to Reading Pennsylvania.

When we were told we would be moving to Reading Pennsylvania, it was a surprise. My entire life was spent in Coatesville, and my plans were to complete Junior High School, and attend Scott High School. We had relatives living in Reading, and visited a couple of times a year, but living there was another story. My mother was looking forward to the move, as she had never lived outside of Coatesville. I was attending the seventh grade at a brand new school, South Brandywine, and did not want to leave.

However, our opinion did not count and we were unceremoniously moved to Reading. My father said that he would be commuting the thirty miles from Coatesville every day, but that did not happen. He kept his job at Lukens Steel Mill, and showed up less and less. This was after our two older brothers left for the Military, and he was hitting forty. There was less time for sharing between my mother and I, and the conversations about our ancestors ceased.

My mother eventually got a job working at a Nursing Home and things were looking up for a while. Dad was still working, but had gambling debts, and owed every paycheck. There was one time when he came home and threw money in the air after winning. Within a week, he was gone with his left over winnings and mom's paycheck. It was probably part of his mid life crisis, but in the end, it cost him his life. By the time, he was diagnosed with cancer he was terminal, and it ravaged his body. He died two days before his fifty-first birthday in May of 1971. I prefer to remember my father during the first twelve years of my life, when we were a family.

There were some good times in Reading, which is a quaint city made up mainly of Row houses. It was supposedly the Pretzel Capitol of the World, but it should have been the Beer Capitol of the World. There were several large breweries in the center of town, with beer flowing on the ground. Reading was a Manufacturing Center, with factories that produced clothing from head to toe, including underwear and women's Lingerie. Luden's Candy was a huge factory in the center of town, and left a chocolaty smell in the air. Chocolate in Candy is addictive, but while it is being processed, it is bitter and stinks.

The Junior High Schools in Reading were harder to get used to, especially with the closed campus. In Coatesville the Junior High School, South Brandywine was brand new, and out in the country, with grass and fresh air. Besides the basic studies, we had Art and music classes, played field hockey and had archery classes. The schools in Reading were more like prisons, then places to learn.

My sister and I attended Southwest Junior High School, and then transferred to Southern Junior High, which was a little better. When the bell rang, everyone ran up or down the stairs headed for class. I did not know there were stairs you were only supposed to go up, and others you were only supposed to go down. The Hall Monitor stopped me, and admonished me for going up the down stairs. That was my introduction to an Urban School, and it only went downhill from there.

There were Italians, African Americans and Hispanics, but Reading was a predominately a Polish, German, and Dutch City. There were Beer Breweries, Candy Companies, and Pretzel Factories throughout Berks County. Anything that could be manufactured was, and that included, clothes, shoes, and Purses. The manufacturing whether Candy or Clothes was by and large, owned by someone who was Dutch or German. Other than Luken's Steel Mill, The little shops in Coatesville paled in comparison to the Manufacturing in Reading Pennsylvania.

The relationship with my mother was strained while we lived in Reading, as we struggled to survive. The most hurtful part was that my mother seldom shared stories about our family history once we were in Reading. As the years passed Coatesville, and childhood seemed like a distant memory. When my father was diagnosed with Cancer, things went from bad to worse. He died of cancer in June of 1971, at the Veteran's Hospital in Dover Delaware. In June of 1972, the remnants of our family left Pennsylvania, and headed for Oakland California.

In 1972, Oakland California, was the home of the Black Panthers, and bordered on Berkeley. It was like being on another planet, filled with peace, joy, and love. No one was thinking about the past, only living for each day. Most of the African Americans in the San Francisco Bay Area came from Texas, Louisiana, or Mississippi. We share a common heritage and experiences through the history of our ancestors in America. These differences made me want to go back and learn more about our family history. By 1978 my mother and I were starting our project to document her family, beginning with the Oral History. Little did we know that the task would stretch out over thirty years, and reveal an amazing history.

⌘ ⌘ ⌘

CHAPTER TWO

≠ ≠

SOME HISTORY OF THE SOUTH CAROLINA BAXTER & BONAPARTES

The Orangeburg South Carolina Baxter's, were probably slaves of John Baxter, who according to the Census for 1850 was a Planter in South Carolina. Our South Carolina Baxter lines go back to a William Baxter, who was born about 1840 in Orangeburg South Carolina. We believe he is Grandfather Charles Wesley Baxter's Grandfather. The family believes that William served in the Civil War; however, we have not located his records. The family elders say that his wife Mary Jane (maiden name unknown) tried, on more than one occasion, to collect his veteran's benefits; lacking appropriate documentation, she was not successful.

When my brother, Dr. Anthony Baxter, took a male line DNA test, to trace our Paternal Baxter line, the results were Native from Columbia South America. They may have been the Taino's who occupied most of the Caribbean including, Puerto Rico and Cuba. Until my brother took the DNA test, there was a rumor that the Baxter's were Native. Now we know that it was not just a rumor.

BAXTER PATERNAL LINE DNA - HAPLOGROUP K (M9)

Haplogroup K is a lineage defined by a genetic marker called M9. This Haplogroup is the final destination of a genetic journey that began some 60,000 years ago with an ancient Y chromosome marker called M168. The very widely dispersed M168 marker can be traced to a single individual- "Eurasian Adam." This African male, who lived some thirty-one thousand to seventy-nine thousand- years ago, is the common ancestor of every non-African persons living today. His direct descendants migrated out of African and became the only lineage to survive away from humanities' home continent.

Some ninety to ninety-five percent of all non-Africans are descendants of the second great human migration out of African, which is defined by the (DNA) M9 Marker. Most residents of the Northern Hemisphere trace their roots to this unique individual, and carry his defining marker. Nearly all North Americans and East Asians have the (DNA) M9 Marker, as do most Europeans and many Indians. The Haplogroup defined by K (M9), is known as the Eurasian Clan."[2]

This ancestor traversed throughout Asia, and into South America, over thousands of years. They were the ancestors of the Arawak people of Columbia South America.

"Approximately 1,500 years ago, the Arawak people of South America began migrating northward along the many scattered islands located between South and North America, an area we now refer to as the Caribbean. For a thousand years, their population grew and the people lived in harmony. The people covered all the islands of the Caribbean, the major ones, as they are now known: Cuba, Puerto Rico and Hispaniola as well as all the smaller ones: the Bahamas, Bimini, Jamaica etc. Certain groups of island people identified themselves as Lokono, Lucayan, Carib, Ciboney, Arawak, but most islands were primarily inhabited by people who called themselves Taint, which stood for "the good people" in their language. The different groups intermarried extensively to strengthen ties amongst themselves."[3]

WILLIAM BAXTER, GREAT-GREAT GRANDFATHER

William Baxter is probably the Grandfather of Charles Wesley Baxter, and would be my Great-Great Grandfather. William was born into slavery in Orangeburg, South Carolina about 1840. Although we have yet to confirm his service, some of us believe that William Baxter was a Civil War Veteran: The family elders say that his wife Mary Jane (maiden name unknown) tried, on more than one occasion, to collect his veteran's benefits; lacking appropriate documentation, she was not successful.

Although this is not clear in documentation, we are probably descendants of William's wife Mary Jane, who was born in 1845. I say "possibly" because Charles's father Isaiah Baxter was born around 1860. It is possible that Mary Jane was his mother, although, at the time of Isaiah's birth she would have been about 15. We have documented at least eleven other children of William Baxter, some of who died young and some of who are possibly unknown branches of the larger William Baxter Clan.

"Isaiah Baxter married Emma Boyd (I note here that some in the family believe that Emma's maiden name was not Boyd but Cheese borough). They believe that, after her parent's premature demise, young Emma went to live with the Boyd's, her Cheeseborough Family relatives; she later adopted their name). Both Isaiah and Emma died between 1890–1900 of a condition known as dropsy. Isaiah and Emma had at least eight children: Charles, Lemuel, David, Artimus, Mary, Olive, Lonnie, and John.

After Isaiah and Emma died, the younger children went to live with various relatives, in Orangeburg and St. Matthews; Charles (b. 1878; d. 1954)) married Annie Rebecca Bonaparte (b. 1892; d. 1968) in or near Orangeburg, SC (some say in St. Matthews, SC) in 1912 and migrated North in 1923 to Coatesville, PA. Annie was the daughter of Isaac and Adriana Darby Bonaparte. Annie had four siblings: Jeremiah, Napoleon, Jin, (or Jinsey), and Perline (died in 2007).

Charles and Annie Bonaparte-Baxter had fourteen children: Alonzo (deceased), Isaac (deceased), Rubelle (deceased), George (deceased), Belgium (deceased), Emma, Samuel (deceased), John, Ada, Lenore, Solomon, Dorothy (deceased), Evelma (deceased), and Milton.[4]"

Grandfather Charles Baxter came to Pennsylvania from South Carolina in 1920. He left his position as a sharecropper and came north to work in Lukens Steel Mill. His mission was to save money, and send for his wife Annie, and their four children, including my father, George Baxter. There was little time to waste and none was wasted, as it only took him two years to send for his family. He promised his wife Annie he would send for her, and the children, and kept that promise. According to my mother, going back was out of the question, as he had left owing money to the owner of the farm he sharecropped. The song that Billie Holliday sang titled, "Strange Fruits," was reality in 1920's, Orangeburg, South Carolina.[5]

Grandfather Baxter was a tall brown-skinned man, who was always smiling, and pleasant. His job on Saturday's and Sunday mornings was to clean the streets of South Coatesville. He pushed a wheelbarrow up the street, picking up trash along the way and whistling the entire time. Some mornings I listened for his whistle, and ran outside to join him as he cleaned the streets. He would wait for, and take my hand as we went down the Avenue, towards Coatesville proper. We walked all of the way down the Avenue, past our church, and almost to Lukens' Company Store. Near Lukens' Store, we would turn around and back to my house, where I received a shiny nickel. I still dream about walking down the street with Grandfather Baxter, pushing his Wheelbarrow, and whistling down the Avenue.

When I was about eight years old, we went to our Grandparents house down the hill, and all of our relatives were there. It was somewhat strange to see everyone there, including our Aunts, Uncles, and Cousins from out of town. We, the younger children, were in a room playing, when a loud wail went up. One of our Aunts' came into the room and said that Grandfather Baxter, had passed away, and we cried. Later that week, a viewing was held in the living room, something commonly done in the south. Life went on and soon we only had the stories to remember him by, but he is not forgotten.

BAXTER AND BONAPARTE – ORANGEBURG COUNTY SOUTH CAROLINA

Some of our South Carolina family surnames are, Baxter,Bonaparte, Darby, Wright, Boyd, and Cheeseborough. Most were slaves, in and around Orangeburg County, and surrounding counties. When one of my paternal Aunts' took an mtDNA test, we found that our Grandmother Annie Bonaparte's, maternal lines, originated in Northern Nigeria. Her mother's name was Adrianna Darby, and she married Isaac Bonaparte.[6]

The tribe she came from is the Fulani, which is in Northern Nigeria and still in existence. The Fulani were scattered throughout, Puerto Rico and the Caribbean during slavery. The name of my Paternal Grandmother's mother was Adrianna Darby-Bonaparte. Her husbands name was Isaac Bonaparte, and that is about as far as I got with that line, although many Bonaparte relatives continue to live in Orangeburg South Carolina.

They would most likely have been Taino's, the Natives who inhabited the Caribbean Islands and South America. The first Natives Columbus saw on the island of Haiti were the Taino. About fifty years later the population was virtually decimated due to disease and wars. The Taino were a culture that had thrived for thousands of years until after the landing of Columbus in 1492.

Grandfather Baxter received a fourth grade education at the African Methodist Episcopal (AME) Sabbath School in South Carolina. After the Civil War, Sabbath Schools were opened in Black Churches throughout the south. It was there he learned reading, writing, and arithmetic. He remained as a member of the Bethel AME Church, even though his wife and children attended the Church of God in Christ. Our house on South First Avenue was next to Bethel AME Church. Their service was more subdued then the services at the Church of God In Christ. It gave me a different perspective from the singing and shouting in our holiness church. It was just as quiet as the church we attended (Church of God In Christ), was loud.

According to my brother Ronald, our South Carolina Baxter relatives, owned homes, farms, and business and were self-sufficient. After joining the Air force, he traveled there, the first one of our generation to do so. He enjoyed going there because they treated him like the long lost relative that he was. He also got tips on farming and told us that they were growing Soy Bean.

LEONARDO BELLAMY ON SOUTH CAROLINA BONAPARTE LINE

"The furthest we have been able to go back is to May of 1819 the birth date of my Great Great-Great-Grandfather, Wynard Bonaparte, whose wife was named Eve. Finding his parents, would put us into the 1700's and possibly closer to understanding how/when we came to South Carolina. He was born in Jamison South Carolina and Elloree County area of South Carolina. He moved to St. Mathews South Carolina in his early adulthood.

Amazingly, given the time period with White Supremacy at its height, Wynard owned over 150 acres of land. He was an industrious farmer and blacksmith, the stories on him are amazing. He made yokes for oxen out of wood and collars for his mules out of corn shuck and cow hide. He made rims for wagon wheels, shoes for mules & horses, and various devices to beat and grind rice like the pestle. He was said to have been very independent and we believe that's how he was able to acquire all this land."[7]

We continue to look for Baxter and Bonaparte ancestors, and descendants, and to learn about this part of our family history.

⌘　⌘　⌘

CHAPTER THREE

⇗ ⇗

GRANDMOTHER CLAN THE GREAT VALLEY'S ORIGINAL PEOPLE

"While many blacks are aware of Native Americans in their family trees, few know the extent of the relationship. Slaveholding brought rigid stratification to the previously fluid Native American society and helped weave racial prejudice into the fabric of Indian Communities." William Loren Katz

Doing genealogical research to find your ancestors, requires many skills, one of the most important being a knowledge of history. This chapter's importance is in the history of the Native People, who lived Pennsylvania's Great Valley. The answer to who my ancestors were was not more than a stones throw away from where I was born. The history of the Great Valley includes Coatesville, which is located in the Great Valley.

The names of our Native Ancestors, who inhabited the area, were lost to us. An important part of the history of Natives is written in the land they lived, and its preservation. The plant and animal life, streams, rivers, and plant life, were plentiful when the Europeans arrived. Native history remains, in the trees, caves, rivers, and the earth they maintained, and left in pristine condition.

The Great Valley encompasses Pennsylvania, Delaware, and parts of New Jersey. The first people of the area were Natives who are now lumped together as Delaware Indians, and resided there for thousands of years. They constructed Wigwams along Rivers and Creeks, in the area. The Natives lived throughout the Eastern Shore of Maryland and Virginia; as far North as Canada; as far South as Tennessee; and as far East as New Jersey. It is interesting to note that Natives were in the Great Valley longer than Christianity has been a religion. In 1682, a part of the Great Valley was formed into Chester County, by Europeans, and became one of the original counties in Pennsylvania.

The Indians were not counted in 1799 when the first census was taken in Chester County. By that time, most of their lands were confiscated, and they, by either death, or assimilation, were displaced. They may not have had grand buildings, but they left a pristine environment, for those who followed. The Europeans found fertile farmland, fresh air, and clean water, on which to build their culture.

GEOGRAPHICAL NAMES OF CHESTER COUNTY

No one seems to have thought of retaining the names given by the Indians as a rule, and hence the map of Chester County contains very few aboriginal names. The list appears to comprise but three names, — Octorara, the meaning of which is unknown; Pocopson, which signifies brawling or rapid stream; and Toughkenamon, signifying Fire-Brand Hill. Of the streams, the Indian names borne by many of them, besides the Octorara and Pocopson, are given on ancient maps; thus the Christina was called Minquas; the Elk, Sickpeckon; White Clay Creek, Swapecksisko; Red Clay Creek, Hwiskakimensi; Chester Creek, Mecoponacka; Darby Creek, Mohorhootink; and the French Creek, Sankanac.

The Indian name of the Brandywine below the forks is not certainly known. It is spoken of by tradition as both Suspecough and Wawassan. One of the branches of it was called by the Indians Chichokatas, as is shown in a deed from James Harlan to James Gibbons, dated 4th month 7, 1731, for five hundred acres of land, described as "lying and being upon a Branch of Brandywine called Chichokatas," on which he (Harlan) then lived, in or near Nantmeal. On old maps the Brandywine is called Fish Kihl (Swedish) and Bränwin's Creek.

It (The Brandywine), most probably derived its name from one Andrew Braindwine, who at an early day owned lands near its mouth. It was very common in the olden time in the lower counties, as they were called (now the State of Delaware), to name streams after the dwellers upon their banks. This creek is shown by the old records to have been known as the Fishkill until the grant of land to Andrew Brandywine in 1670, immediately after which it is referred to on the records as Brandywine's Kill, or creek, and the name was eventually corrupted into its present form of Brandywine.

The Natives from Southeastern Pennsylvania were hunter-gatherers and moved from Village to Village. The Indian Tribes inhabiting what is now Chester County were, when the country was first settled, known collectively as the Lenin Lenape, but were generally called Delaware by the settlers. They lived in small tribes, generally occupying the tributaries of the Delaware, and each tribe was frequently known to the settlers by the name of the stream it occupied. The tribe, which occupied the region drained by the Brandywine, was known as the Nanticoke.

These tribes each had their own Sachem or King. The name Lenni-Lenape signifies "Original People," a race unmixed and unchanged. The word Lenape is properly pronounced in three syllables, Len-a-pe. When the name was changed to "Delaware" was first applied to them, they thought it was given in derision; but were reconciled to it on being told that it was the name of a great white chief, Lord De la Warr. As they were fond of being named after distinguished men, they were rather pleased, considering it as a compliment.

They were more thickly settled in some portions of the county than others were. Along the Great Valley, and in the Region of Pequea, Lancaster County, they were numerous; in other parts of the county they were more evenly distributed, except west of White Clay Creek, where they are said to have been rather sparse. Their Wigwams were generally clustered five or six in a place, on the south sides of the hills, and near springs of water. Some of these clusters were of considerable size, and known as Indian Towns or Villages.

There were a considerable number of these in the county; one of them stood on the farm late of John R. Kinsey, deceased, in Upper Oxford Township and another in London Britain Township, near the Baptist Church. Their usual employments were hunting, fishing, manufacturing baskets, and cultivating small patches of Indian corn. They had paths leading from point to point, some of which afterwards became public roads for the settlers. One of these paths, extensively traversed, led from Pequea, where they had a large settlement, to the headwaters of the Chesapeake Bay.

It ran on the ridge dividing the waters which flow into the Delaware from those, which flow into the Susquehanna, and in its whole course did not cross a single stream of water. The path is now what is known as the Limestone Road, running from the Pequea Valley through the townships of Sadsbury, Highland, West Fallow field, Upper and Lower Oxford, and East Nottingham, and into Cecil County, Maryland.

They had also a village or town, consisting of about thirty Wigwams, near two fine springs at what is called Indiantown, in Wallace Township. They had abandoned to some extent nomadic habits, raised some corn and tobacco, and planted fruit-trees. Their principal subsistence, however, was obtained by hunting and the catching of fish, which were abundant in the Indian Run and the Brandywine.

When Daniel and Alexander Henderson purchased the land, in 1733, on which the town and burial-ground of the natives were placed, they promised them that the latter should never be disturbed. This promise was faithfully kept by them and their children. It is now part of a cultivated field. This graveyard occupied a little more than a quarter of an acre, and contained about one hundred graves. These Indians removed shortly after Braddock's Defeat, when the feeling against the natives was bitter, to what is now Crawford or Mercer County, in this State.

About the year 1697— fifteen years after the arrival of William Penn— a tribe of the Shawnees, or Shawnees, came from the southward, and desired leave of the Conestoga Indians, and of Governor Markham, to settle on Pequea Creek, which was granted, the Conestoga Indians becoming security for their good behavior. These Shawnees, or Shawanese, Indians extended their settlements within the present limits of Chester County.

They had a large town about where the Village of Doe Run now stands, where seems to have been the council-house of the nation; and they also settled in considerable numbers in the neighborhood of Steeleville, on the Octorara Creek. A Tribe of Indians known as the Okehockings were originally seated near Ridley and Crum Creeks, within the present limits of Delaware County. About 1701 they were removed, by direction of William Penn, to another tract higher up on Ridley Creek, which had been granted to Griffith Jones, but given up by him."[8]

There is the saga about, "Indian Hannah," who was the "last," Indian in Chester County. It did not occur to the historians that the Natives were hiding in plain site, afraid of being sent West on the, "Trail of Tears." The newly arrived settlers were passing laws against Natives forbidding them to fish or plant corn. Not obeying the law meant going to jail, and/or losing their land. Many went deep into the Appalachian Mountain Range, and hid there for generations. In Southeastern Pennsylvania, the Natives hid in the Welsh Mountains, along with escaped slaves, and poor whites, who were disenfranchised. The Appalachian Mountain Range traverses the region as far south as Tennessee, and as far north as new York.

Indian Hannah seems to be Chester County's version of Pocahontas. She is described as being friendly with the whites and left her own people to live among them. My theory is that she left her people to live on the land her ancestors occupied for thousands of years. She may have been designated as the, "Keeper of the Spirits" of the ancestors.

Indian Hannah. She lived in the area known as Kennett Square, with a white family. The story she tells gives insight into how the original inhabitants of that region lived. To make the record clear, she was not the last Indian in that area, but the last Indian identified by European Settlers. Many of her tribe had scattered to Delaware and other areas, after the incursion of Europeans.

She was called Hannah Freeman; just as freed slaves took on European Surnames, so did Hannah. My interest in her is that she lived in the same area, where my Native Ancestors lived in Newlinville. That is where her family planted Corn. She dictated her life story to Moses Marshall, the overseer of the poor for Chester County, on July 28, 1797. Marshall was interviewing her to determine which township in Chester County should be responsible for her support, so the story focuses primarily on her family, places of residence, and employment.

"The examination of Indian Hannah, (alias, Hannah Freeman); who saith that she was born in a Cabin on William Webb's place in the township of Kennett about the year 1730 or 1731. The Family consisted of her Grandmother Jane and Aunts Betty and Nanny. Her Father and Mother used to live in their Cabin at Webb's Place in Kennett in the winter and in the summer moved to Newlin to plant Corn—she was born in the Month of March. The family continued living in Kennett and Newlin alternately for several years after her birth as she had two brothers born there younger then herself. The Country was becoming more settled and the Indians were not allowed to Plant Corn any longer; her father went to Shamokin and never returned.

The rest of the family moved to Centre in Christiana Hundred, New Castle County and lived in a Cabin on Swithin Chandler's place. They continued living in their Cabins sometimes in Kennett Square and sometimes at Centre till the Indians were killed at Lancaster (1765), soon after which, they being afraid, moved over the Delaware, and then to New Jersey. There they lived with the Jersey Indians for about Seven Years after which her Granny Jane, Aunt Betty, and Nanny (her Mother), and Self came back. They lived in Cabins sometimes at Kennett (Square) at Center at Briton's Place and at Chester Creek occasionally as best suited.

This mode of living was continued until the family decreased her Granny died abt. [ove] Schuylkill her Aunt Betty at Middletown, and her Mother at Centre. She lived about two years worked at Sewing and received three/six [three shillings, six pence] per week wages. She worked a few weeks in some other places at Gideon Gilpin then went to her Aunt Nanny at Concord.

Nevertheless, having almost forgot to talk Indian and not liking their manner of living as well as white peoples, she came to Kennett Square and lived at William Webb's place. She worked for her board sometimes but got no money except for baskets, besoms, etc. She lived at Samuel Levis three years that is made her home and worked sometime, and received for her board no wages, but made baskets. She stayed the longest where best used but never was hired or received wages except for Baskets."[9]

Hannah lived as her ancestors had for thousands of years, and refused to separate herself from the land. Her family were intact until forbidden from planting corn, (the main food staple), when the father left. They were forbidden to grow corn, and the fields went fallow, so of course the father left. Then the land was given to a European Settler, who more than likely grew corn. One of the main staple crops grown in Chester County is corn and it was a cash crop for many years.

Indian Hannah's Village was in the same area where three generations of our Martin Ancestors lived. There were several recorded generations of Martin's who lived in Newlinville, in an area known as Doe Run. They moved back and forth from Lancaster County to Chester County beginning in the 1700's. According to my mother an Indian woman married, a white man named Charles Martin (in the 1700's). By that time, they identified themselves as Mulatto in the census records. In Chester County, there was an Indian Village in the area now known as Newlinville.

INHABITANTS OF THE WELSH MOUNTAINS

The Appalachian Chain of mountains extends through the eastern territory of the United States from the Saint Lawrence River on the north to the State of Georgia on the south. The greatest heights are in North Carolina. There they are between 6,000 and 6,800 feet above the sea. This conspicuous chain includes all the ridges; and two ridges extend through Berks County. They are the Blue Mountain and the South Mountain.

The Blue Mountain, in its course south twenty-five degrees west from the Delaware at Easton to the Susquehanna (River) at Harrisburg, forms the present northern boundary line of Berks County. It was a barrier to migration in the earliest settlements of this section of the State and it was the limit of the earliest surveys, which were made northwestwardly from the Delaware River.

Its average height above the sea is about 1200 feet. The distinguishing peculiarities in the formation of the mountain in Berks County are the "Pinnacle," the "Schuylkill Gap," the "Round Head" and numerous ravines which were washed out in the mountainside by rolling waters in the course of time, and came to be useful to man in having marked out for him easy passes over the mountain. From a distance, the rounding has a bluish appearance. Hence, it was and is called Blue Ridge. On one of the early maps, it is called the "Kittatinny Mountain," corrupted from the Indian word Kau-ta-tin-chunk, meaning endless. It is also sometimes called North Mountain."[10]

My mother described our Native and Free Black ancestors as coming from the Welsh Mountains. The Welsh Mountain Range runs through several Pennsylvania Counties, including Chester, Lancaster, Delaware, Dauphin, and Berks. The trails leading from the south into Pennsylvania were used by the Natives for thousands of years. Over many generations of isolation and intermixing, in the Welsh Mountains, a rugged group of Tri Racial Isolates was formed. They did not have a lot of material wealth, as the air, earth, land, and sky were their wealth. This land has now been lost as the older residents die off, and the counties stepped in to claim the land.

The Nanticoke tribe originally occupied the area between the Delaware and Chesapeake Bays, in what is today Maryland. After the British conquest of the east coast, the tribe was granted a reservation near the Nanticoke River, but the British soon disbanded it and forced the Nanticoke's off the land. Some Nanticoke people fled north to Pennsylvania or joined the Delaware on their westward migrations to Ohio, Indiana, Oklahoma, and Ontario, Canada. Other Nanticoke remained behind in their traditional territories.

Dispossessed and isolated, the Nanticoke Tribe were known for sheltering escaped slaves during the early days of American history—one 18th-century recording of "Nanticoke" vocabulary turned out to be Mandinka, a West African language! After emancipation, many Nanticoke passed as black, or sometimes as white if they were mixed-race, but despite losing their language and much of their culture, other Nanticoke people have maintained their heritage to the present day.

The land hungry European immigration of the seventeenth century disrupted the Native American communities. Implicit in these attempts to get land was the ethnocentric attitude of the Europeans who viewed Native Americans as inferior, and therefore felt little guilt about taking their land, or their lives. The wars and diseases brought to the Natives, by settlers, resulted in the demise of tribes and villages. Many of the surviving descendants of the Delaware were scattered, and forced to relocate during the, "Trail of Tears." Those who remained in the area were racially designated as Mulatto, White, or Colored.

MORE ABOUT THE GREAT VALLEY REGION

The Great Valley, also called the Great Appalachian Valley or Great Valley Region, is one of the major landform features of Eastern North America. It is a chain of valley lowlands — and the central feature of the Appalachian Mountain system. It stretches about seven hundred miles from Canada to Alabama and has been an important north-south route of travel since prehistoric times. Native Americans created the trails through the Great Valley, over thousands of years. In pre-colonial and early colonial times, a major Indian Pathway through the Great Valley was known as the Great Indian Warpath, Seneca Trail, and various other names.

For White Immigrants the Great Valley was a major route for settlement and commerce in the United States, along the Great Wagon Road, which began in Philadelphia. In the Shenandoah Valley, the road was known as the Valley Pike. The Wilderness Road branched off from the Great Wagon Road at present-day Roanoke Virginia crossed the Cumberland Gap and led to Kentucky and Tennessee, especially the fertile Bluegrass Region and Nashville Basin. Another branch at Roanoke, called the Carolina Road, led into the Piedmont Region of North Carolina, South Carolina, and Georgia.

The various gaps connecting the Great Valley to lands to the east and west have played important roles in American History. On the east side, the wide gap in Southeast Pennsylvania became the main route for Colonization of the Great Valley. By the 1730s, the Pennsylvanian Great Valley west of South Mountain was open to settlement after treaty cessions and purchases from the Indians.

The area became known as, "The Best Poor Man's Country," many of those who moved into the mountains (white, black, and native) formed Isolate Communities. Before long immigrants had thoroughly settled the Great Valley in Pennsylvania and were rapidly migrating and settling southwards into the Shenandoah Valley of Virginia.

The entire region between Southeast Pennsylvania and the Shenandoah Valley soon became famous as a "breadbasket," the most productive mixed farming region in America. The road from Philadelphia west to the valley and then south through it became very heavily used and known variously as the Great Wagon Road, the Philadelphia Wagon Road, the Valley Road, etc.

SUSQUEHANNA RIVER

"One of the great wonders of the Chesapeake Bay Watershed is that you can stand in Southern New York State and place a small wooden boat in one of the tributaries of the Susquehanna River and follow it into and through the Chesapeake Bay and then out into the Atlantic Ocean."[11]

This area extended throughout Eastern Pennsylvania, Delaware, and New Jersey. The Natives moved around the area freely, sometimes following game, and other times farming fertile ground. There is no accurate count of how many Natives inhabited a particular area, prior to European Colonization. When the Delaware Indians were in Chester County, they tended to settle around Streams and Rivers there. Some like the Susquehanna retained the original name of the rivers.

LIFE WITH THE LENAI-LENAPE

The Lenai-Lenape are a deeply spiritual, and held belief in a Creator, and lesser Gods, which reached all aspects of their lives. Their beliefs are reflected in a deep reverence for the natural environment, and a concept that humans are only a small part in Nature's grand scheme. This belief made it difficult for them to understand the concept of land ownership and purchase..[12]

The Lenai-Lenape believe in an afterlife, but without the Christian concept of heaven and hell - a source of considerable frustration for Moravian Missionaries. Lenai-Lenape were reluctant to tell their real name, and the use of nicknames was very common. The real name of Captain Pipe, the head of the Delaware Wolf Clan in 1775 was Konieschquanoheel "maker of daylight." His nickname, however, was Hopocan meaning "tobacco pipe" - hence his historical name of Captain Pipe.[13]

NATIVE SPIRITUAL PRACTICES

Native Spiritual Beliefs, in Southeastern Pennsylvania, were developed over thousands of years. There was no large building which was attended on a certain day of the week. The beliefs were based on a reverence for life, the ancestors, and nature. Often times the Natives practiced their beliefs in the caves in the area. There is the Crystal Cave, which is located in Berks County. Throughout the Welsh Mountains Caves which were used by the Natives for spiritual and burials exists. In Native belief animals are seen as cousins, the earth our mother, and Great Spirit the father. Males and females have their place in the life cycle, and neither is more or less than the other. This view of life contrasted with Europeans, who believed in land ownership, and that they were dominant over the earth.

There was no concept of land ownership, or the, "Rugged Individualism" of Europeans. The tribe was more important then the individual in native and African Cultures. In Lanai Lenape customs, Religious Ceremonies were centered on a dedicated "Big House." Dreams were considered very significant, so Lenape Priest were divided into two classes: those who interpreted dreams and divined the future; and those dedicated to healing. The dead were buried in shallow graves, but methods varied considerably: sometimes flexed, extended, or individually, and sometimes in groups.

Some Martin's are listed as Indian Traders along with the Clouds, who were also in Chester County. They moved around, and were in New Jersey, Delaware, and Maryland. When Penn settled Pennsylvania, he talked about the Indian Traders, who were in the West Marlboro Area. One of those traders was George Martin, who married Rachel Cloud. The Clouds were also Indian Traders, who settled in and around Chester County.

According to my mother, Great-Grandfather William Martin was an overseer on a large Ranch at Doe Run. The owner of the ranch was Buck and Doe Run Valley Farms, Inc and was owned by the King Ranch. He also worked for Maurice Darlington for many years, keeping up his properties. Although he lived in Chester County, Grandfather Martin spent his summers with relatives who lived in the Welsh Mountain area of Lancaster County. The Welsh Mountains encompassed several counties, including Berks, Chester, Lancaster, and Dauphin. My mother grew up on a farm in Coatesville, which was located on Goose town Road.

Grandfather Charles Martin spent a lot of his growing up years in the Welsh Mountains with our Green relatives. The surnames of some of the Lancaster County relatives are Martin, Boots, Green, Harris, and Parker. That is where he learned the fine art of making "Corn Liquor," and how to use herbs to heal. The main ingredient in Corn Liquor was of course Corn, and Chester County had plenty of that.

"Indians and people with Indian Heritage have always lived in Pennsylvania and continue to do so. According to the 1960 U.S. Census, one thousand and twenty-two Indians lived in Pennsylvania. In 2000, the U.S. Census counted 18,348 American Indians or Alaskan Natives living in Pennsylvania, as well as another 34,302 people claiming such heritage in combination with one or more other races.

As these statistics indicate, the Native American population of Pennsylvania is growing, a result of migration into the state and an upward trend in the number of people identifying their ethnicity as all or in part Native American. Unlike most states, Pennsylvania may not have any formally recognized Indian Reservations within its borders, but Indian Identity persists among its inhabitants, constantly adapting and reinventing itself in the modern age."

⌘   ⌘   ⌘

CHAPTER FOUR

⚡ ⚡

PEQUEA VALLEY ROOTS MARTIN FAMILY LINES

"Yet few Black Americans realize that their familial ties to Native Americans are evidence of an important historical process. When Europeans first arrived in what would become Latin America, they enslaved the native people. The Indian populations fell victim to overwork, disease, and deliberate extermination."[14]

Pequea Valley was part of the Great Valley, in Chester County, until the formation of Lancaster County in 1729. This is where the Conestoga Indians lived and flourished until the settlers arrived. In order to understand how they lived, it was necessary to understand what the area looked like prior to Colonization. There were brooks and streams running throughout the area, which emptied into the Delaware River. The fact that Natives preserved their habitat for thousands of years without polluting the earth, and air, says a lot about their reverence for the environment. Instead of building cement and brick houses, they built earth friendly structures.

The great flats of Pequea, on which king Tanawa resided, presented the appearance of a cultivated meadow surrounding the several Indian Cabins. All was stillness not a sound to disturb the general. The great flats of Pequea were natural meadows on which grass grew luxuriantly, which proved a great source of comfort to the new settlers. The Indians were scattered along the banks of the Pequea, every wigwam being governed by a chief who was subject to Tanawa. The chief knew William Penn, and called him the 'Indians' friend. He frequently reminded the settlers of the promise made by William Penn, the great father from the wide waters, when they intruded upon his rights."[15]

The Pequa Valley Indians were called Conestoga, and were part of the Iroquois Confederation. There are not many written testimonies of these people, and their lives. They seem to be like ghost, once there and now gone, replaced by a foreign people. The available information refers to the Delaware and Iroquois Confederations. The Conestoga (Kanastóge, 'at the place of the immersed pole') was an important Iroquoian tribe that formerly lived along The Susquehanna River and its branches in what is now Lancaster County.

Although William Penn and the Natives had a friendly relationship, other Immigrants to the Valley did not share those feelings. A series of massacres took place against the Conestoga Indians in 1765, which, along with disease, affected their demise. The Lenai-Lenape are known as the "Original People," or "Men of Men," and sometimes referred to as the "Grandfathers." The Nanticoke are known as the "Tidewater People."

In the Great Valley, our Martin, Green Nocho, and Page ancestors were remnants of the tribes, which congregated in Delaware, New Jersey, Maryland, and Pennsylvania, and as far north as Canada. With the intermarriages and mixing of the races, some Natives became white and others, Negro, Mulatto, Colored or black.

ANCESTORS IN THE GREAT VALLEY

Great-Great Grandfather Uriah Martin was born about 1835, the son of Charles and Sarah Johnson-Martin. He was born in West Marlboro Township of Chester County, as was his father, Charles Martin I, (born about 1810). In the 1860 Federal Census, Charles Martin I, Uriah's Father, states that his parents were born in Pennsylvania. In that Census Uriah's age is listed as twenty-five years old, and he is living with is father. By 1870, Charles Martin is living in Chester County, in West Marlboro Township. Charles, Uriah, James, and Susan (Charles second wife), all list their race as Mulatto. Uriah States in his Civil War Pension file, that his parents were Charles and Sarah Johnson-Martin, who were born in Chester County.

The Civil War Pension Application for Great-Great Grandfather, Uriah Martin contains a wealth of genealogical information. There is a notation that his birth year was included in a family Bible, and that there were thirty-one notations of birthdates. This Bible proved our connection to the Johnson, and Martin Families, who were often, spoke of by my mother. In 1811, Sarah and her brother Elijah lived in Charlestown Township, which is near present day Phoenixville. I was able to find her father, Elijah Johnson, who was one of the settlers of Liberia (West Africa), and is written about in another chapter.

Uriah Martin's Civil War Pension Application also contained his wife, Tamyzine Page-Martin's name, and stated that she was born in Pennsylvania. The Federal Census for 1850, for the County of Lycoming, City of Muncy Pennsylvania, lists a Terenemah Page. She is the daughter of George and June Page and her birth year is 1838; the same year Tamson Page was born. In the 1870 Federal Census for Chester County, the birthplace of the parents of Tamyzine listed as Pennsylvania. The document filled in some of the missing pieces of the oral history of our maternal lines. Mom said that some of our Pennsylvania relatives were Natives who lived in the Welsh Mountains. According to my mother, our ancestor, Tamyzine Page-Martin was a Mohawk Indian from New York.

Recently Cousin Louise Hinton stated that our Great-Grandmother Lydia Green-Martin had a picture of an Indian Chief in Full Headgear. She stated that Grandmother Lydia Martin told her he was a relative, but she does not remember his name. Cousin Louise Hinton lived with our Great Grandparents, William, and Lydia Green-Martin, when she was a child. My maternal Grandparents, like many from their generation, had two generations of children; consequently, I have first cousins my mother's age.

They lived in the same area as the Nochos, who are cousins, and of partial Native Ancestry. The Nochos were described by my mother as Natives who were her cousins through our Martin Family. She stated that her cousin, Leon Nocho often came to visit the family when she was a small child. He was described as copper colored with long black hair, and of thin wiry build. In the 1900 Federal Census for Chester County, Johnnie and Leon Nocho are listed. They are living in the household of Uriah Martin, in West Marlboro Township.

Cousin Louis Nocho and I exchanged information about our families and he was able to shed light on their family history. The Nocho family lived in the area of Lancaster County known as Pequea Valley, before moving into Oxford. Johnnie Nocho and Philena Martin were married sometime in 1894. The couple died leaving two sons, who were raised by Uriah Martin. The Nocho Family lived in the same area as the Martins, throughout Chester and Lancaster County, in Delaware, and New Jersey. The Hosanna Church Cemetery at Lincoln University in Chester County contains headstones with the names of Nocho and Hilton.

There were not a lot of identifiable Natives around Pennsylvania when I was growing up. We had cousins, who my mother stated were Native, and lived as either white, or African Americans. Most of the relatives in our community attended Christian Churches, and with the exception of my mother, did not talk about their histories. The ones that were in our family did not openly identify themselves as Native, or state which tribe, they came from. Finding a tribe in Pennsylvania was not as difficult as finding the individual within the tribe.

The records of Native names prior to being christened are not readily available. In order to find the individual it is necessary to trace the Christian (or European), name, which goes back to the 1600's (in some cases). There were Natives adopted or fostered out to white families, and they too were given European Surnames. In my family, several Martin male ancestors have the name of William Penn, including my Great-Grandfather, William Penn Martin. Pennsylvania's founder, William Penn was widely perceived to be a friend and savior to the Indians, especially the Conestoga Indians. He may have had a fondness for the Natives, but those who followed were not as caring.

NOCHO MARTIN CONNECTIONS – CHESTER & LANCASTER COUNTY

In 1850, there were five Noker men in Salisbury Twp., Lancaster Co., PA. Jacob, John and Hiram were all living in Edward's household in 1850 as young single men; Edward was married with a family; Samuel was married with a family and also living in the township; all five were listed as laborers and as "mulatto", and were probably brothers.

In the 1860's Hiram and Samuel owned property in close proximity near Limeville in Salisbury Twp. , where John was a quarryman, and Hiram was a farm laborer with $400 worth of real estate. Their surname has been spelled various ways in the official records—the earliest census record (1820) lists the name as Noka but the various records eventually settled on Nocho. I am guessing, because many of the variants have a hard "k" sound in the middle, that the family pronounced their name "Noe-koe," rather than "Noe-choe."

The parents appear to have been John and Mary. In the 1820 U.S. census for Caernarvon Township, Lancaster County, PA, John Noka is listed as a Free Colored Person (FCP) engaged in manufacturing, age 27-45. The rest of his household was also listed as FCPs:

1 adult female: age 27-45
4 males under 14
1 male 14-26
2 females under 14

Sometime around 1894, Johnnie Nocho married Philena Martin, the sister of my Great-Grandfather, William Martin. They had two sons Leon and Johnnie Nocho, who were orphaned at a young age, and raised by their Aunt and Uncle William and Lydia-Green-Martin. My mother describes her cousin Leon Nocho tall and skinny, with Copper colored, and with long black hair. She also said that the Nochos were Indians and like the Martin's had come from the Welsh Mountains.

DAVIS/GREENS FROM DELAWARE TO PENNSYLVANIA

Lydia Davis married George Green on 10 Sep 1834, in Sussex County Delaware and they are listed in Delaware Marriages 1645–1899. Lydia Davis-Green was my Great-Great-Great Grandmother, and lived in Chester County with her daughter Susan Green (my Great-Great Grandmother). Susan Green was married to Henry Green, who does not appear to be a close relative. In fact, as a child, Susan was living with a Green Family in Lancaster County, and she was the only one listed as being born in Delaware. At the time, her mother, Lydia Davis-Green, was a live in domestic in Chester County.

In the 1930 census for West Chester, George Green (son of Susan Green) is listed as the stepfather of Thomas J. Henson. There may be a trail that leads from LaPlata and Port Tobacco in Charles County MD, right up to West Chester. A cropping of "Dent" headstones at the Chestnut Grove Cemetery in West Chester gave me a clue as to the relationship between the Dent and Henson's. I found Jennifer Rustin living near Dent's and Henson's, and some other familiar names, down in LaPlata and Port Tobacco last century. The Rustins are the family of Bayard Rustin, who my mother stated was our cousin.

Great Grandfather William Martin worked for Maurice Darlington for over thirty years. It appears that William and Maurice Darlington were employers of many blacks in Chester County. William Darlington, lived in Ercildoun first, and then moved to West Chester, and his son Richard had a seminary in Ercildoun, which was also moved to West Chester at some point.

Several family members worked for William Darlington, including, Maria and Samuel Rustin, and Julia Davis

Charles and Leah Ruth-Martin were married on October 26, 1904, by William O. Jones. They had children Pearl, Sarah, Ruth, Lydia, Clifford, Samuel, Charles Junior, Vivian, Ramona, Dorothy, and Cora. Charles Senior and the family owned a Farm in Honey Brook, and later on Goose town Road in Coatesville. On the marriage certificate, Charles Martin is listed as being born in Doe Run, and Leah at Erculdon Pennsylvania. They probably met at the Church of Christ, where Samuel Ruth, Leah's father was a Minister.

Mom (Verna Vivian Martin), was born in 1923, and was the seventh child born to the couple. In the 1930 Federal Census, Charles Martin is listed as the head of his family, in Honey Brook, Chester County Pennsylvania. He lists his occupation as Auto Mechanic, and the census states that there was an Auto Repair Shop, located on the property. He was probably the first Car Dealer in Chester County, and owned several cars from the Ford Motor Company. According to my mother Grandmother Leah Martin, was the first woman to have a Drivers License in Pennsylvania. Grandmother Leah Martin drove A-Tin Lizzie Car, straight from the Ford Automobile Assembly line.

Mom said that they usually vacationed on the Eastern Shore of Maryland, before her parents separated. They owned a boat, which was towed to the Eastern Shore of Maryland. There are varying stories about Grandfather Charles Martin selling liquor during the Roaring Twenties and beyond.

A story that my mother often recounted was of Elliot Ness on his way to arrest her father (Charles Martin), and got a flat tire. Grandfather Martin agreed to repair the tire, if they would not arrest him. He fixed the tire, and Elliot Ness did not arrest him, at least not that night. My mother said that they had parties at the house every weekend that lasted all night, and that Grandfather Martin sold liquor. Other people in the community have also attested to him selling Corn Liquor. Some of the older people in the community said that his place was hopping, every Saturday night.

There is a, "Violation of Liquor License Code," against Grandfather Martin, and Walter Ruth, his brother-in-law. Grandfather Martin pleaded guilty and served a six-month sentence, while Walter Ruth stood trial and was found not guilty. In 1943 there was a "Petition for Destruction of Liquor" issued to Grandfather Martin. The Liquor Control Board sent a, Special Deputy Attorney General, from Philadelphia to oversee the destruction. The order was signed May 28, 1943, and delivered to his Warehouse, which was located on Gap Road in Coatesville. Grandfather Martin owned Warehouses throughout Lancaster and Chester County Pennsylvania.

During the roaring twenties, illegal Liquor Stills were prevalent, throughout the county, especially in rural areas. Grandfather Martin was brewing his own Corn Liquor, and beer, in conservative Chester County. The farm he owned had animals, and large crops of corn, which was used to make the Corn Liquor. My mother stated that there were ten children, and numerous other relatives, and farm hands living at their farm.

The Martin Line is one of the most complicated to unravel, because of the racial mix. Near Coatesville there is an area called Martin's Corner, where four generations of Martins lived. They were my Grandfather, Charles Martin II, his father, William Martin, his father, Uriah Martin, and his father, Charles Martin I. Charles Martin I, was born about 1810 in Chester County, probably at Doe Run.

Our first male Martin ancestor in Chester County was probably a white male, who was married to an Indian woman. The Free Octorara Church was set up for the Colored members to attend. The Graveyard contains surnames such as, Martin, Davis, and Thompson, all of whom are related.

Census and Church records are important tools in researching your ancestors. These records often contain information on birth, deaths, marriages, and Christening. In the 1840 census for Chester County, I found an ancestor, Charles Martin I, who was identified as a Mulatto. In the 1850 census for Colerain Twp., in Lancaster County Another ancestor, Benjamin Green, is also identified as a Mulatto. Benjamin's wife, Sarah is identified as white on that census and the children as Mulatto.

Through my maternal Grandfather, Charles Martin we connected with the Natives and whites in Lancaster and Chester County Pennsylvania. Several were Tri-Racial Isolates from the Pique (Pequea) Valley, which at one time covered the entire Great Valley Region, and is now located in Lancaster County. In other words they were mixed raced, Native/African/Whites. Those with ties to the area call it, The Welsh Mountains. It was common knowledge in Coatesville who the mountain people were in the community.

Following are some listing for our family's ancestors who resided on the border of Chester and Lancaster County. The listings show the areas where they lived, age, occupation, and race. It is interesting to note that the race started as Mulatto, and changed to black. There were no cases of the race changing from Mulatto or black, to white.

CENSUS LISTINGS FOR GREEN, MARTIN, & NOCHO SURNAMES

1840 Upper oxford Twp., Chester Co., PA
MARTIN, Charles, 3 males under 10, 1 male 24-3, 1 female under 10 and 1 female 24-36
1850 Colerain Twp., Lancaster Co. PA
GREEN, Benjamin , 60, Mu, Laborer, PA
GREEN, Sarah , 44, W, PA
GREEN, Effa , 44, W, PA
(Living in separate households)
BAILY, Obed Baily, Head of Household
MARTIN, Charles Marton (Martin), 42, Mu, Laborer, PA
MARTIN, William, 17, Mu, Laborer, PA
MARTIN, Uriah , 15, Mu, PA
MARTIN, Phirenah, Mu, PA
1850 Salisbury twp., Lancaster Co., PA
GREEN, Benjamin Green, 25, Mu, Laboreer, PA
GREEN, Catherine Green, 24, Mu, wife, PA
GREEN, William, 4, Mu, PA
GREEN, Benjamin, 3, Mu, PA
GREEN, Samuel, 1, Mu, PA

GREEN, Henry, 22, Mu, Laborer, Pa
GREEN, Elizabeth, 15, Mu, wife, PA
GREEN, Mary, 2 months, Mu, PA
1860 Sadsbury Twp., Lancaster Co., PA
MARTIN, Charles, 50, Bl, (no occupation), Pa
MARTIN, Susan, 38, Mu, DE
MARTIN, Uriah, 25, Bl, PA
MARTIN, James, 3, Mu, PA
MARTIN, Mary E. 9 months, Mu, PA
PAGE, Tamson, 20, Mu, Domestic, PA
1860 Colerain Twp., Lancaster Co., PA
GREEN, Benjamin, 70 Mu, (no occupation), PA
GREEN, Sarah, 55, W. PA
GREEN, Amanda, 17, W, PA
GREEN, Harrison, 13, W, PA
GREEN, Henry, 13, Mu, PA
Marlborough Twp., Chester Co., PA 1870 West
GREEN, Henry, 42, Bl, (Farmhand), PA
GREEN, Susan, 33, Bl, PA
GREEN, Nathan, 15, Bl, PA
GREEN, Lydia A., 13, Bl, PA
GREEN, Charles , 9, Bl, PA month, Bl, PA
MARTIN, Uriah, 32, Mu, Quarryman at Limestone Quarry, PA
MARTIN, Tamyzine, 28, Mu, PA
MARTIN,William P., 8, Mu, PA
MARTIN, Henry, 6, Mu, PA
MARTIN, Philena, 4, Mu, PA
MARTIN, Anna F., 8 months, Mu, PA
1880 West Marlborough Twp., Chester Co., PA
GREEN, Susan, 43, Bl, W, h of h, DE DE DE
GREEN, Charles N., 18, Bl, son, PA PA PA
GREEN, Sarah E., 12, Bl, dau, PA PA PA
GREEN, George, 9, Bl, son, PA PA PA
GREEN, Clara, 7, Bl, dau, PA PA PA
GREEN, Lydia, 72, Bl, mother, widow, DE DE DE servant
MARTIN, Uriah , 54, Bl, Laborer, PA PA PA
MARTIN, Tamyzin, 34, Bl, wife, Keeping House PA PA PA

MARTIN, William, 18, Bl, son, laborer, PA PA PA
MARTIN, Harry, 16, Bl, son, laborer, PA PA PA
MARTIN, Anna, 10, Bl, dau, servant, PA PA PA
MARTIN, Mary B., 4, Bl, dau, PA PA PA
MARTIN, Jacob B., 1, Bl, son, PA PA PA

1880 Colerain Twp., Lancaster Co., PA
GREEN, Benjamin, 56, Bl, Farmer, PA PA PA
GREEN, Catherine, 56, Bl, wife, PA PA PA
GREEN, Charles, 9, Bl, grandson, PA PA PA

1900 PA West Marlborough Twp., Chester Co.,
GREEN, Charles N., Bl, b-October 1862, 37, m'd 10 yrs, day laborer, PA PA PA, rents house
GREEN, Mary E., Bl, b-February 1868, 32, wife, 7 children, 5 living, PA PA PA
GREEN, Ella E., Bl, b-September 1887, 12, daughter, PA PA PA, at school
GREEN, Florence A., Bl, b-December 1889, 10, daughter, PA PA PA, at school
GREEN, Clarence H., Bl, b-June 1893, 7, son, PA PA PA, at school
GREEN, William M., Bl, b-November 1894, 5, son, PA PA PA
GREEN, Sarah J., Bl, b-June 1898, 1, daughter, PA PA PA
GREEN, Susan, Bl, b-April 1833, 67, widow, 8 children, 5 living, PA PA PA, servant, rent house.
GREEN, Sarah E., bl, b-August 1877, 32, daughter, PA PA PA, servant
GREEN, Clara M., Bl, b-September 1877, 22, daughter, PA PA PA, servant
GREEN, Hannah A., Bl, b-Mach 1832, 68, widow, aunt, PA PA PA
MARTIN, William P., Bl, b-May 1862, 38, m'd 19 years, PA PA PA, farm laborer, rent house
MARTIN, Lydia A., Bl, b-December 1861, 38, 2 children, 1 living, PA PA PA
MARTIN, Charles F., Bl, b-January 1886, 14, son, PA PA PA, at school
DAVIS, Horace, Bl, b-February 1890, 10, nephew, PA PA PA, at school

GREEN, George, Bl, b-September 1872, 27, single, PA PA PA, farm laborer

1900 East Marlborough Twp., Chester Co., PA

MARTIN, Jacob, Bl, b-September 1878, 21, m'd 2 yrs., PA PA PA, day laborer

MARTIN, Tillie, Bl, b-February 1878, 22, wife, 0 children, PA PA PA

MARTIN, Uriah, Bl, b-August 1837, 63, widower, Father, PA PA PA, day laborer

MARTIN, Blanche, Bl, b-December 1887, 13, sister, PA PA PA, at school

NOCHO, Leon, Bl, b-August 1896, 4, nephew, PA PA PA

NOCHO, Johnnie, Bl, b-July 1897, 3, nephey, PA PA PA

Following is an excerpt from an article on the Welsh Mountains:

"For generations, descendants of Indians, escaped slaves, and early pioneers mingled in isolation there. Stories spread legends persisted…, Night comes suddenly to Welsh Mountain. One minute, the reddening western sky eerily illuminates the rectilinear fields of corn, tobacco and alfalfa nurtured by Amish and Mennonite farmers in the valley below…,

There were few places in America where the Melting Pot boiled more fiercely than here, and the result was a society of ragged, rugged individualists, who lived in interracial harmony while the more advanced societies below them drew color lines and lynched and looted and burned. The skin coloring of Welsh Mountain's interracial families alternated between generations –light-skinned parents would give birth to dark-skinned children."[16]

The memory of the breathe taking beauty of those mountains stay with me. Although it is called a mountain, the area is more hills and valleys, rising no more than one thousand feet at its highest point. What made it seem like a mountain were the ancient trees, which towered over the area. There was a mist coming off the trees that gave the place a mystical look. That is how I remember the mountains, and the people living there were just as mystical as the mountain. Many were poverty stricken, and forced into the valley below to look for work, or attend school. Most have died off and the land has been confiscated, and developed, by the counties that adjoin the mountains (Chester, Dauphin, Lancaster, and Berks).

I have communicated with a descendant of Abe Buzzard who lives in New England, and we traded wonderful stories. She had articles, which mentioned my Green ancestors, and stories of the infamous Buzzard Family. It was a wonderful feeling to have reached over the years and connected with another descendant. The woman I communicated with was well educated and we exchanged information about our ancestors. Although the Buzzards were a gang to those in the Valley, some mountain folks spoke fondly of them.

After serving in the Civil War, Great-Great Grandfather, Henry Green, and his first wife Susan, separated, and moved to Mount Airy in Lancaster County. When he applied for a Civil War Pension, he was living with Carolyn Harris (his second wife), and they had several children. Grandfather, Charles Martin spent his youth, hunting and fishing, in the Welsh Mountains with his Green, Boots, and Parker cousins. Some of the surnames of my Pennsylvania family members are Johnson, Martin, Green, Boots, Parker, Thompson, Pennington, Nocho, Johnson, Middleton, Craig, and Bowman's' were some of the surnames from that area. There is a lot of intermixing and marrying over the generations, and I can find a cousin almost anywhere throughout Chester and Lancaster County.

THE FALLEN - NATIVES IN LANCASTER COUNTY PENNSYLVANIA

There were two subjects I did not hear a lot about in school, one was the contribution of Native Americans, and the other was contributions of African American (in the 1950's and 60's), and slavery. What I have learned is that once the Indians were converted, their voices were silent, a deathblow to a people who had such a strong oral tradition.

For the Susquehanna, although the tribe ceased to exist, their legacy remains with the descendants who can still trace their lineage to the once-powerful confederacy, and with the name that will never be forgotten. As long as the Susquehanna River flows to the sea, we will remember the Susquehanna. The last massacre of Indians in Pennsylvania was carried out in Lancaster County (in 1765), by a gang of thugs known as the Paxton boys.

The Paxton Boys were a militia in Pennsylvania, who were no they were the fore runners of the Ku Klux Klan. in Pennsylvania. They visited the same terror on Pennsylvania Indians, which would later be visited on blacks. The Paxton Boys was an organization based in Paxton Township near Harrisburg, and then considered the western frontier of Colonial Pennsylvania.

They were primarily made up of Scotch – Irish who had settled in the region. This group did not face well-armed Indians, instead they went after old men, women, and children, when they were alone and vulnerable. They have been described variously as frontier militia, vigilantes, thugs, and backcountry farmers. Although most colonists were appalled by the massacre of the innocent and peaceful Conestoga, the Paxton Boys suffered no legal consequences of their action.

MURDERED AT CONESTOGA TOWN

Sheehays	Ess-canesh. (son of Sheehays)
Wa-a-shen (George)	Tea-wonsha-i-ong (an old woman)
tee-Kau-ley (Harry)	Kannenquas (a woman)

MURDERED AT THE LANCASTER WORKHOUSE

Kyunqueagoah (Captain John)	Ex-undas (Young Sheehays, a boy)
Koweenasee (Betty, his wife)	Shae-e-kah (Jacob, a boy)
Tenseedaagua (Bill Sack)	Tong-quas (Chrisly, a boy)
Kanianguas (Molly, his wife)	Hy-ye-naes (Little Peter, a boy)
Quaachow (Little John, Capt John's son)	Saquies-hat-tah (John Smith)
	Chee-na-wan (Peggy, his wife)

Ko-qoa-e-un-quas (Molly, a girl)Karen-do-uah (a little girl)
Canu-kie-sung (Peggy, a girl)
Indian Survivors on the Farm of Christian Hershey
Michael   Mary (his wife)

"Those who cannot remember the past are condemned to repeat it." George Santayana - Poet

⌘ ⌘ ⌘

CHAPTER FIVE

⚡ ⚡

A PRESIDENT IN THE FAMILY

"In 1639 three Indentured Servants in Virginia tried to flee the oppression of their servitude. One was a Scotsman, one an Englishman, and one, John Punch, was African. When they were captured, the Virginia Court sentenced the Scotsman and Englishman to serve an extra three years on their indentures. In the first ruling of its kind, the Court sentenced John Punch, the Black Man, to life-long servitude. Thus, Three hundred and sixty nine years ago John Punch became the first African Slave in American history.

Tonight, Three hundred and sixty nine years after the John Punch incident, America elected Barack Obama its forty-fourth President. It has taken us three hundred and sixty nine years to travel from slavery to freedom, from the most wretched human condition to the weal of political power. Tomorrow the struggle begins anew; but tonight, let us celebrates the great victory that brings us the wonderful opportunity to struggle on!" Dr. Anthony Baxter on the Presidency of Barack Obama.

This is the eve of the election of the first African American President of the United States, Barack Obama. This is the manifestation of the words spoken by America's Founders, although they may not have ascribed it to an African American President.

America's founding fathers wrote and spoke of freedom, and inalienable rights. Those words rang loud and clear, and planted the seed of a movement. Our leaders continually quote the words of the founding fathers, and each generation passed those words on. The result is the first African American President, and a new day for all Americans.

It was an awe-inspiring experience to see people all over the world cheering America, and Barack Obama. There were people of all races, thousands, upon thousands, waving cheering this man. Now President Obama has a Multi-Racial Heritage, and a diverse upbringing. His first book, Dreams From My Father: A Story of Race and Inheritance inspired me to continue to write about and document my family history.[17]

Barack Obama's father is of Kenyan Descent, and his mother is White American, possibly of English and Irish Descent. They are the parents of our President Barack Obama, the first African American President in our Countries history. America has labeled him African American, and experiences good and bad, are based on that premise. He has broken through the glass ceiling, to become the leader of the most powerful country in the world. My family ancestry, like many Americans and Barack Obama's, is mixed raced and diverse. We are the, Pieces of the Quilt, which make up the fabric of America.

These days, there are few African Americans, who are pure African, although we are generally lumped together. There are three identifiable racial groups worldwide, Asian, African, and European. The subgroups are mixtures of the three primary groups, and are ethnically diverse. African Americans, and Hispanics, are more of an ethnic group, than a racial group, and are diverse in many ways. There is no definitive term on race as humans have traveled all over the globe intermixing, and or adapting to their environment.

The label of Latin Americans was given to South Americans who were colonized by Spain. The Country of Brazil was a former Colony of Portugal, and is culturally different from other parts of South America. However, there may be racial similarities with Indians in Brazil and other parts of South America. When slaves were brought to the America's they were taken to Puerto Rico, Panama, Cuba, Brazil, and Islands throughout the Caribbean. These days choose a race or ethnicity is left up to the individual, and in most cases not in the hands of the government.

THE PRESIDENT IN OUR FAMILY – ELIJAH JOHNSON

Elijah Johnson is my direct ancestor, through my Maternal Grandfather's line. Grandfather Charles Martin I, was the son of , William Martin, who was the son of, Uriah Martin, the son of Charles and Sarah Johnson-Martin. As a child, Sarah and her brother (Elijah) lived in Charlestown Township, in Chester County. The children attended the Poor Children's school in Chester County, starting about 1816. In 1819, Sarah and Elijah Junior were residents of the Poor Children's Home, in West Chester. The records of the Chester County Archives, list the children's father as Elijah Johnson, a Negro. There is no mention of the mother, who by then may have been deceased.

Elijah Johnson Senior may have been away fighting, or studying for the ministry, when he and the children were separated. By the time he left for Liberia in 1820, he was remarried with two children. My ancestor's mother may have been deceased by that time, and left the children with relatives who were not able to support them. Elijah Johnson was not listed as living in the Poor House, and was probably not the person who left them there.

Directors of the Poor and the Chester County Poor House

The Chester County Poor House was erected for the support of the poor in the county. The Directors were responsible for providing for the lodging, maintenance, and employment of the poor. Those who had money in Colonial Pennsylvania were largely landowners, and/or who owned businesses. Very few of the Free Blacks, or other People of Color, had either, and most lived and worked on farms.

Sarah and Elijah Junior, the Johnson Children, were nine and eight years old respectively, when attending the Poor Children's School. They were taught to read and write, and if left too long, they were apprenticed out. Elijah Johnson Junior was indentured out, and Sarah eventually left the facility. Within a few years Sarah

Johnson was married to Charles Martin I, and living in the West Marlboro Township of Chester County (according to the 1840 census). She was deceased by 1850, when Charles was living alone with his minor children. By 1860, Charles was living on the farm of Obed Bailey, with his children and new wife, Susan.

The Martin and Johnson Family lines connected about 1830, with the marriage of Charles Martin I, and Sarah Johnson. They were the parents of my ancestor Uriah Martin, who was born August 11, 1835, in Chester County. He had two brothers, William and James, and two half-siblings. Uriah's Civil War Pension file application, lists his mother's name as Sarah Johnson, and states that she was born in Pennsylvania.

OUR LIBERIAN CONNECTION

"Abolitionists may talk twaddle till the crack of doom, but after all, Colonization is to be the great cure of Negro slavery in this country, or it remains uncured. You may free the slave in the South, but he is nevertheless a slave North or South. His shackles are only to be cast off by returning to the land of his ancestors. Here he is surrounded by a wall of prejudice as indestructible as the everlasting hills. The fires of the volcano are not more inextinguishable than this prejudice, and we would therefore remove the black man from its influence, instead of encouraging him to break it down by an insolent bearing towards those who are in ninety-nine cases out of a hundred, his intellectual superiors."

Newspaper Editorial, West Chester, Pennsylvania, 1854.

Elijah Johnson was born about 1789 in Virginia, and as a child moved with his family to New Jersey. He was in New York when the War of 1812 broke out, and he joined the cause. He served with Hall's Regiment during that war, in the fight against the British. These events took place around the time my ancestor Sarah Johnson and her brother Elijah Junior were born. Sarah Johnson, Elijah's daughter, was born about 1808 and her brother Elijah about 1810. Getting from New York to Pennsylvania required no more than taking a boat down the Susquehanna River.

He may be a descendant of Antonio Johnson, the first Negro to land at Jamestown Virginia in 1619. Antonio Johnson fought for and won his freedom, and was the first black person to do so, in Colonial Virginia, He and his wife, Mary, lived on the Eastern Shore of Virginia, before moving into Maryland. He had about several children who were scattered throughout Virginia, Maryland, and Delaware. The descendants spread throughout New Jersey, Pennsylvania, and Ohio prior to the Civil War.

In 1820, Elijah and eighty-six others emigrated to Liberia, on the Ship Elizabeth. They landed on Sherbro Island in what is today Sierra Leone. Elijah's wife Mary and many others died of Malaria and Yellow Fever. In 1821, the surviving settlers moved to Providence Island near what is today Monrovia. There, he married Rachel Wright, with whom he had several additional children, including Hilary Johnson, who would become the eleventh President of Liberia in 1884.

The group could not have foreseen the fate waiting them in Liberia, nor the history they were about to make. After the death of many of the ships passengers, they were faced with the prospect of returning to America. Instead, they went to an area now known as Monrovia Liberia, and along with other survivors, built a city. The British offered military assistance to the settlers in, and Elijah Johnson declined the offer, with a "No Thanks."

As a Soldier and Methodist Minister, in America, Elijah Johnson was gone for extended periods. He was a Missionary Minister, who traveled to remote areas to Preach. As a Methodist Minister, Elijah left his Liberian family for long periods. As a Methodist Minister even in Liberia, he was in the bush preaching. In the book, Power and Press Freedom in Liberia, 1830-1970, it states that, "As a child Hillary (Johnson), saw little of his father, who spent much of his time away as a Methodist Minister, to the Gola and Kpelle."[18]

Elijah was a colonial agent of the American Colonization Society in Liberia. He served in this role from June 4, 1822, until August 14, 1823, when he was replaced by Jehudi Ashmun. In 1847, he was one of the signers of the Liberian Declaration of

Independence. He died in 1849 in White Plains, a missionary station in the interior of Liberia. He was not at home with his wife and children, but in the Bush with the Natives. Elijah did not amass a fortune in Liberia, nor leave his family well off.

"In 1816, a group of prominent political leaders, seeking to end slavery, began urging the emancipation of slaves on the condition that they emigrate to Africa. They formed the American Colonization Society (ACS), and six years later, the society established the Colony of Liberia on the West Coast of Africa. By 1867, the ACS had sponsored more then thirteen thousand Free Black Emigrants into Liberia."[19]

The Liberian and American descendants of Elijah Johnson have similar names for their children. It appears that Elijah Johnson Junior is the only child named after his father. My ancestor, Sarah Johnson-Martin died before 1850, when her son Uriah was about fifteen. There was a listing for an Elijah Johnson living in Pennsylvania, but he is listed as a white man. If this is his son than his family is not aware (or ignoring), the fact that he was a Person of Color.

Many of the Liberian Descendants of Elijah Johnson now live in the United States, and we have communicated. Great-Great Grandfather, Uriah Martin's name always intrigued me, as no one else in the family, had that name. One of my Liberian Cousins states that there was an Urias Johnson in their family. We did a lot of comparing of names and dates, and will be meeting to do even more.

Regardless of what side of the fence one falls on, we should understand those who were seeking freedom. Some People of Color, saw no possibility of freedom in America, while others vowed to stay and fight. Native Americans were leaving America, and settling in Mexico and Canada, in an attempt to escape persecution. Many records are available in Canada, and America, for researchers whose ancestors emigrated out of America.

FIRST NATIVE BORN PRESIDENT OF LIBERIA

Hillary R. W. Johnson was the son of Elijah Johnson (Senior), whose daughter Sarah Johnson-Martin is my direct ancestor. He was the eleventh President of Liberia, and the first Native born President of that Country.

⌘ ⌘ ⌘

CHAPTER SIX

⁓ ⁓

MYTHS AND TRUTHS ABOUT THE UNDERGROUND RAILROAD

Slavery existed in Pennsylvania from a very early period, having been first introduced by the Dutch and Swedes, prior to the granting of the province to William Penn. As early, however, as 1712 an effort was made to restrain its increase by the passing of an act by the Colonial Assembly to prevent the further importation of Negroes into the province. This law, however, from commercial considerations, and regardless of the dictates of humanity or the best interests of the province, was subsequently repealed by the home government, which had a veto upon the acts of the Colonial Assembly.

Some years subsequently another act was passed, imposing a prohibitory duty on their introduction, but this also was repealed by the Crown. England at that time pursued the traffic in Negroes with eager avarice. Those imported into Pennsylvania were chiefly from the West Indies, as it was found that in transporting negroes from Africa directly to the more northern provinces, their health suffered more than when gradually acclimated by being taken first to the West Indies and thence farther north. The price of an imported Negro man about the middle of the last century was £40, Pennsylvania currency, and from that upwards to £100.

It is not known when slavery ceased to exist in Chester County by the death of the last slave, but it must have been many years since, as none was slaves for life who were born after March 1, 1780.[20]

The Underground Railroad was neither Underground, nor a Railroad. It was in fact a system of safe houses for escaped slaves who were seeking freedom. Despite the stories of secret hiding places, exciting rescues and railroad terms such as 'stations', 'passengers', 'conductors', and 'presidents' of the underground line, there was no organized system and most slaves planned and conducted their own escapes with little help.

The history of the Underground Railroad has been written from accounts left by abolitionists, and agents, such as Harriet Tubman, and William Still. There were also Vigilance Committees formed in some northern communities who provided food, temporary housing, travel directions, and sometimes transportation to slaves who passed through their communities. Chester County was one of the most important stops on the Underground Railroad for many freed slaves.

Most accounts and stories of the Underground Railroad underplay the role of Natives and blacks. The role of Indians in assisting slaves escaped is seldom mentioned in history books, yet they were the first to point slaves north. They were in fact targeted because of the assistance they offered slaves seeking freedom. The trails leading north were paths taken over thousands of years by Native Americans. They assisted slaves in escaping and in some cases allowed escaped slaves to hide on their Reservations.

Natives were brought and sold just like slaves, and they too made use of the Underground Railroad. In fact, Natives and Africans were in the same boat, whether escaping slavery, or forced removal. Natives were heading for Canada, escaping massacres and forced removals. The newspapers had accounts of Natives being bought and sold, and of their running away; as in the other colonies, the leading men of the colony owned them.

Penn's own deputy, Governor William Markham, owned one who was born in 1700, and by the terms of Markham's will, was to be freed at the age of twenty-five. In a bill of sale of the personal effects of Sir William Keith, dated May 26, 1726, an Indian woman and her son were mentioned among the seventeen slaves listed [21]

"As the result of the intermingling of Negroes and Indians, which came about when the coast tribes dwindled and the small number of remaining members moved inland, associated and intermarried with the negroes until they finally lost their identity and were classed with that race, a considerable portion of the blood of the southern negroes is unquestionably Indian. [22]

It was these mixed bloods, as well as the pure blood Indians, to which the statutes referred by the terms "Indian slaves" and "Mustee," or "Mestee," slaves. Occasional mention is made in the colonial newspapers of slaves of the mixed red and black races.[23]

The opinion has even been advanced that, in certain of the colonies, there never were any Pure blood Indian Slaves. Mr. W. B. Melius of Albany, New York, asserts; "I do not believe the pure Indian was sold as a slave (in New York). I believe the Indian who was the slave was not without mixture." [24]

Harriet Tubman - Known as "Moses," after the biblical hero who delivered the Hebrews from slavery in Egypt, was the most famous conductor of the Underground Railroad. Born into slavery in Dorchester County, Maryland, Tubman fled to Pennsylvania in 1849. After freeing herself from slavery, this abolitionist returned to Maryland and rescued members of her family and others. It is believed that she made nineteen trips into the South and, over a period of ten years, conducted approximately three hundred people to freedom in the North without ever losing any of her charges.

During the American Civil War, Tubman moved to South Carolina where she served as a nurse, scout, and spy for the Union Army. She also helped prepare food for the 54th Massachusetts Regiment, a heroic band of African-American soldiers who were known as the "Glory Brigade" after the fierce battle at Fort Wagner in 1863. She was never paid for her services, but she received an official commendation for her war effort. [25]

Leaders of the Underground Railroad Movement published their memoirs and provided facts for northern newspapers, after the Civil War, highlighting their role in the Underground Railroad Movement. The role of Africans themselves, who were enormously courageous and followed their own plans to escape enslavement, is often overlooked. The Underground Railroad helped slaves to reach freedom, usually after the most dangerous part of their journey was completed. Harriet Tubman, led many to freedom, but there were also slaves who escaped and made their way to freedom on their own. Yet she influenced others with her brave escapades into the southern states, and her legendary and heroic deeds.

WILLIAM PARKER AND THE CHRISTIANA RESISTANCE

"The legacy of William Parker is one of heroism. However, for current scholarship, William Parker and the Resistance of Christiana had almost been lost to the history of African-Americans. He is mentioned, but rarely as the hero of the resistance, in historic annals. White observer Castner Hanway, not William Parker, was portrayed as the hero of the event. David Forbes, a Quaker, wrote in 1898 that Hanway was, "the hero of the riot, by reason of his Trial for Treason."

The stone monument, which stands at Christiana to commemorate the resistance lauds Edward Gorsuch as, "dying for the law," and Castner Hanaway who, "suffered for freedom." William Parker is a nondescript name lost in the category of names indicted for treason. His name is listed as number thirty.

In 1951, when Lancastrians commemorated the one hundredth anniversary of the Resistance, the heroes were still seen as being the white participants. Even African-American speakers applauded the efforts of the white participants. Dr. Horace Mann Bond broached a different hero. He introduced William Parker as a heroic yet tragic symbol of his generation.

"This is the Centennial of the violence engendered by great passions and forces, but also by one man. It is the story of A Man without a Country; it is the tragedy of mankind everywhere who would be free, but must resort to violence to obtain their freedom."

It was William Parkers' house where the incident took place, and his house where the slaves hid out. The plan that was in place to deal with slave catchers was orchestrated and carried out by William Parker and his wife. As the slave catcher argued with Parker, his wife, Elizabeth sounded the alarm, by blowing a horn out of the upstairs window. The mostly African American community responded to the alarm and headed for Parker's house, not knowing who are what they faced. Castner Hanaway was one of those who responded to the alarm, and not the leader. He was there to assist William Parker, and protect the escaped slaves hiding at his house. William Parker took most of the risk, and in fact fled to Canada along the Underground Railroad, after Edward Gorsuch died.

Another leader of the Underground Railroad was William Still, who left his memoirs. He gave a face to the men and women escaping slavery. Following is an account of the Underground Railroad written in his own words.

"Whereas, The position of William Still in the Vigilance Committee connected with the Underground Rail Road," as its corresponding secretary, and chairman of its active sub-committee, gave him peculiar facilities for collecting interesting facts pertaining to this branch of the Anti-Slavery service; therefore Resolved, That the Pennsylvania Anti-Slavery Society request him to compile and publish his personal reminiscences and experiences relating to the "Underground Rail Road."

In compliance with this Resolution, unanimously passed at the closing meeting of the Pennsylvania Anti-Slavery Society held last May in Philadelphia, the writer, in the following pages, willingly and he hopes satisfactorily discharges his duty...,

Occasionally fugitives came in boxes and chests, and not infrequently, some were secreted in steamers and vessels, and in some instances journeyed hundreds of miles in skiffs. Men disguised in female attire and women dressed in the garb of men have under very trying circumstances triumphed in thus making their way to freedom.

Passes have been written and used by fugitives, with their masters' and mistresses' names boldly attached thereto, and have answered admirably as a protection, when passing through ignorant country districts of slave regions, where but few, either white or colored, knew how to read or write correctly. Not a few, upon arriving, of course, had rags enough on them to cover their nakedness, even in the coldest weather. It scarcely needs be stated that, as a rule, the passengers of the U.G.R.R. were physically and intellectually above the average order of slaves. They were determined to have liberty even at the cost of life."

LINCOLN UNIVERSITY AND HINSONVILLE

According to my mother, one of our famous relatives is Matthew Henson, a black man who explored the Artic Region. Matthew Henson was born to in Charles County, Maryland on August 8, 1886. In 1887, Matthew's parents sold their farm and moved to Georgetown, Maryland just outside Washington D.C. It took quite a bit of digging to learn who Matthew Henson was, as the books I read played up Matthew Perry.

He was born around the same time as my grandfather, Charles Martin, and was probably related through, Great-Great Grandmother Susan Green. There are Henson's' listed as living in the same neighborhood as our Green relatives in West Chester. The founder of Hinson Village, Emery Hinson (Henson) is a relative on my mothers' side of the family. He was a free black, who started Hinsonville (now Lincoln University Pennsylvania), by purchasing land where blacks could live. My belief is that he was the Uncle of Matthew Henson, and the brother of the original Uncle Tom, Josiah Henson. Josiah and Emory Henson were both born in Charles County Maryland, and have similar stories. They both settled in Canada, in Free Black Communities.

She said that he had gone to the, North Pole, and had many children there. My mother stated that he came from Maryland, but did not explain how he was connected to Chester County. It was not until 2002 at Lincoln University that some explanation was given. There some of our Bell and Henson cousins told us about Matthew and Emory Hinson (Henson). They are indeed relatives, and are related to Bayard Rustin, another cousin. When Emory Hinson died, he left his land to the builders of what was then Ashmun Institute. I also believe that we are related to Josiah Henson, the character, "Uncle Tom's Cabin," is based on.[26]

All three Henson's (Hinson), were born in Charles County Maryland. Matthew was born after the Civil War, and raised in Washington DC. Emory Henson (Hinson), was born a slave, in Charles County, and escaped first to Chester County, then to Canada. He was instrumental in setting up a community of Free Blacks called Hinsonville, in Chester County on land where, Lincoln University now sits. Hosanna Church, was one of the main stops along the Underground Railroad, and was located in Hinsonville. After Josiah Hinson (Henson) left for Canada, he left half of his land to Ashmun Institute.

Maryland and Virginia were just over the line from Chester County, a line that meant the difference between slavery and freedom. The Underground Railroad offered slaves seeking freedom safe passage to their final destination, whether, Pennsylvania, Ohio, Michigan, or Canada. Once the Fugitive Slave Act was passed (1850), there was no safe haven in North America; escaped slaves headed north, for Canada. The Fugitive Slave Act allowed, Law Enforcement, and Federal Marshall's free reign to capture and return slaves.

In 2002, I visited Hosanna Church in Chester County, and the graveyard there, which contained surnames of Hilton, Nocho, Hinson, and Hill. Hosanna Church (also Hosanna Meetinghouse), and cemetery sits on land now owned by Lincoln University. Hosanna Meetinghouse hosted such historical figures as Harriet Tubman, Frederick Douglass, and William Still.

THE FUGITIVE SLAVE ACT AND THE UNDERGROUND RAILROAD

The Fugitive Slave Act was part of the group of laws referred to as the "Compromise of 1850." In this compromise, the antislavery advocates gained the admission of California as a free state, and the prohibition of slave trading in the District of Columbia. The slavery party received concessions with regard to slaveholding in Texas and the passage of this law.

Passage of this law was so hated by abolitionists, however, that its existence played a role in the end of slavery a little more than a dozen years later. This law also spurred the continued operation of the fabled Underground Railroad, a network of over three thousand homes and other "stations" that helped escaping slaves travel from the southern slave-holding states to the northern states and Canada.

This Act, (law), meant that there was no safe haven for slaves, in America. The Federal Marshall's were required to assist slave owners in capturing escaped slaves. On September 11, 1851, a standoff took place in Christiana Pennsylvania, between a slave owner Edward Gorsuch, and William Parker, a free black. The incident sometimes referred to as the Christiana Resistance, but at the time it happened was, "The Christiana Riot." Edward Gorsuch, his son Dickinson, and a posse showed up at William Parkers' house that day, looking for escaped slaves. Gorsuch was further aggravated by the site of one of his escaped slaves, as he approached the Parker House.

He faced an angry William Parker, and demanded his property. Parker was prepared to defend the escaped slaves with his own life, and an argument ensued. There was an angry exchange, and then gunfire rang out. The bullet hit Gorsuch in the chest, and he fell to the ground, mortally wounded. When the posse looked around, and saw a sea of angry black faces, they ran for the hills.

The Federal Marshall attempted to deputize Castner Hanaway, the only white face in the crowd, but was rebuffed. He was a member of the Anti-Slavery Movement in Lancaster County, and was there to support the Free Blacks and slaves. Parkers' wife,

Elizabeth sounded the horn, summoning those in the community to their house. The goal of the abolitionists in the community was to protect the fleeing slaves. The capture of one slave could compromise the entire movement, which explains why Harriet Tubman carried a gun.

Several of the participants, in the resistance are relatives, including William Parker. Henry Green was one of those arrested and tried for treason with thirty-eight others, including several whites. The blacks were held in a pen in the City of Lancaster; however, they were acquitted of all charges, and set free. William Parker his wife, children, and escaped slaves, fled to Canada, that night along the Underground Railroad. They joined a black community in Canada called, Buxton Twp.

William Parker returned to fight in the Civil War, and afterwards returned to his family in Canada. After the incident at Christiana, thirty-eight men (including my Great-Great Grandfather, Henry Green), were tried for treason and acquitted. William Parker, did not believe that blacks would ever be truly free in America. However, he and his family kept contact with relatives who remained in the area. Even after the Civil War, blacks were leaving the United States and settling in Canada.

The Fugitive Slave Law passed in September 1850, allowed escaped slaves to be captured and brought back to their masters. The law also prosecuted anyone who helped hide slaves or who aided fugitive slaves in any way. The law was expensive to the United States of America, as it cost thousands of dollars to return all slaves to the places from where they had escaped. It was easy to take any Person of Color, free or not and say they were slaves. The Fugitive Slave Law was responsible for the escalation of blacks in Chatham and Buxton Townships in Canada, both of which were final stops on the Underground Railroad.

JOSAIH HENSON IN CANADA (UNCLE TOM'S CABIN)

Uncle Tom's Cabin, situated near Dresden (Canada), provides visitors with a wealth of information about the life

---

of fugitive slaves in the Dresden area. Focusing on the life of Josiah Henson, the site documents his life as a slave for 41 years as well as his life in Upper Canada after escaping from slavery (1830–1883).

The Dawn Settlement, which Josiah Henson helped to settle, began in 1841. It was established to provide a refuge and a new beginning for former slaves. Henson also helped to establish the British American Institute which was one of Canada's first industrial schools. The school was created to advance the plight of fugitive slaves in Upper Canada by allowing them employment opportunities.

Throughout the world, Josiah Henson's name became synonymous with the character "Uncle Tom" in Harriet Beecher Stowe's famous novel Uncle Tom's Cabin when it was published in 1852. During its first year of publication, the novel sold 300,000 copies and dramatically helped to raise awareness with regards to the brutality of slavery. President Abraham Lincoln himself told Harriet Beecher Stowe that he felt that her novel played a role in the onset of the American Civil War and the resulting abolition of slavery.

In 1983, Josiah Henson became the first person of African descent to be featured on a Canadian Stamp and in 1999 the Government of Canada erected a plaque designating him as a Canadian of National Historical Significance."[27]

Josiah Henson, who escaped slavery, is not seen as an Uncle Tom by his family or friends. Uncle Tom would not have escaped from slavery and made his way to Canada. Like many slaves, he may have been appeasing whites who required docility from their slaves. The docile Uncle Tom would not have been instrumental in founding the Dawn Settlement, and setting up a School. South Buxton Ontario Canada-Last Stop on Underground Railroad

In 1849, the Reverend William King and fifteen of his former slaves founded the Canadian Settlement of Buxton on a 9,000-acre block of land in Ontario set aside for sale to blacks. Although initially opposed by some neighboring whites, their town grew steadily in population and stature with the backing of the Presbyterian Church of Canada and various philanthropic.

A developed agricultural community that supported three schools, four churches, a hotel, and a post office, Buxton was home to almost seven hundred residents at its height. The settlement (which still exists today) remained all black until 1860, when its land was opened to purchase by whites. Sharon A. Roger Hepburn's *Crossing the Border* tells the story of Buxton's Settlers, united in their determination to live free from slavery and legal repression. It is the most comprehensive study to address life in a black community in Canada.

South Bruxton is located in Chatham-Kent, Ontario. The last official counting of the population is posted on the sign as you enter. That population is 78. The majority of the population is retirees. South Buxton is home to two roads and St. Andrew's United Church. There is also the well-known South Buxton raceway but it officially lies outside of the village borders. The closest towns are North Buxton and Merlin.

South Buxton was originally known for its role as a large settlement for the end of the underground railroad and the St. Andrew's Church was built by escaped slaves for Rev. William King. The Liberty Bell (a replica was on display at Queen's Park) cast in 1800 was still used to signal the beginning of church service until the 21st Century. The bell originally was rung every time a freed slave reached South Buxton.

THE REVEREND ROBERT A. PINN & THE UNDERGROUND RAILROAD

Over the years I have collected numerous documents on Great-Great Grandfather, Reverend Robert A. Pinn, was involved on the Underground Railroad. The records of his activities are found in the minutes of Monumental Baptist Church, and the Baptist Historical Society. There are not a lot of writings about his activities, and given the times, he may have preferred to remain anonymous. After fleeing Fredericksburg Virginia, he and his family settled in Columbia Pennsylvania. He was born free in a long line of family that appears to have always been free, at least in Virginia. There is still a mystery as to what happened to some of the children. They were listed in the 1860 census for Lancaster County, and never heard from again. They may have died from an illness, or worse yet, been killed in one of the Militia attacks into Columbia.

There is no oral or written record as to the fate of the children, who did not make it to adulthood. After leaving Fredericksburg Virginia in 1853, he and family settled in Columbia Pennsylvania. They lived next door to the Pleasant family in Columbia, just as they had in Amherst County and Fredericksburg. Columbia Pennsylvania, the community they settled in was a hot bed of Underground Railroad Activity. They remained there until about 1860 when he fled to Burlington New Jersey, another community of Underground Railroad Activity.

When the Civil War broke out, Samuel Walter Pinn, the son of Robert A. Pinn, joined the 54th Massachusetts United States Colored Troops, Company B. When the Unit returned from battle, they camped at the home of Reverend Robert Pinn, in Burlington New Jersey. He dedicated his life to Missionary work, and pastured churches in Burlington New Jersey and Philadelphia. After the Civil War, he became the Pastor of Monumental Baptist Church in Philadelphia. There is now a Pinn Memorial Baptist Church named in his honor. Monumental Baptist Church, which was first Primitive Baptist Church, then Oak Street Baptist Church, continues to operate. He lists his occupation as Missionary in the 1860 Federal Census for Columbia Pennsylvania.

His Grandfather, Rawley Pinn was also a Baptist Minister, and preached against slavery. After serving in the Revolutionary War, he founded Fairmount Baptist Church, which continues to operate in Stapleton Virginia. Rawley Pinn's lines were Native/African, and his ancestors were members of the Episcopalian Church in Northumberland County Virginia. The Baptist took hold in Virginia and came under the scrutiny of the Anglican Church for their Anti-Slavery views. This may be why Reverend Robert A. Pinn fled Virginia with his family around 1853.

There is another Robert A. Pinn, who was a Sergeant during the Civil War, and was born in Stark County Ohio, about 1840. He received the Congressional Medal of Honor for his service during the Civil War. He is quite a bit younger then Reverend Robert A. Pinn, my ancestor, who was born in about 1817. The younger Pinn was the son of William and Emily Broxton-Pinn. The father, William Pinn, was an escaped slave from Virginia, where he was born in the household of the Briggs Family. Some family members believe that the younger Pinn is our Great-Great Grandfather, but that has been disproved. The Ohio Robert Pinn died of poisoning in 1911, and had no children. I spent many years researching Sergeant Robert A. Pinn, in the belief that he was our direct ancestor, but his age and location disproved that theory.

He was too young to be our ancestor, and is the same age as the older Robert Pinn's children. He could not have fathered our ancestor, Maria Louisa Pinn, who was born in 1850, when he was born in 1843. His father may have been assisted in escaping from slavery, by our ancestor, Robert A. Pinn. William Pinn, his father, who was a slave, may have been the son of a Pinn (who was free), and a slave woman. After escaping to freedom, he may have taken his father's surname. In Colonial Virginia, where William Pinn was born, any child born to a slave woman was by law a slave. We do believe there is a familial relationship with the younger Pinn, but it has yet to be proven.

ROBERT A. PINN –STARK COUNTY OHIO CIVIL WAR HERO

"Robert A. Pinn (March 1, 1843 – January 5, 1911) was a Union Army soldier during the American Civil War and a recipient of America's highest military decoration—the Medal of Honor—for his actions at the Battle of Chaffin's Farm. Pinn joined the Army in Massillon, Ohio, and by September 29, 1864, he was serving as a First Sergeant in Company I, of the 5th U.S. Colored Infantry Regiment. On that day, his unit participated in the Battle of Chaffin's Farm in Virginia, and it was for his actions during the battle that he was awarded the Medal of Honor six months later, on April 6, 1865. Pinn died at age 67 and was buried in Massillon City Cemetery, Massillon, Ohio."[28]

The Underground Railroad ran throughout the south, along mountain trails, and required a vast network for its success. The preceding is a small part of the history, which deals with that portion running through Southeastern Pennsylvania. There is much more to the movement than depicted here, and there were events prior to and after (such as the Civil War), which were precipitated by the Underground Railroad Movement.

SAMUEL WALTER PINN – A SON & SOLDIER

By the time the Civil War started, Walter Samuel-Pinn, was the only surviving son of Robert and Elizabeth Pinn. He states on his Civil War File, that he was living in Columbia Pennsylvania, and he was a Barber. When the War broke out, he answered a call by Frederick Douglass to join the 54th Massachusetts United States Colored Troops. He trained with the unit in Reedsville Massachusetts under Colonel Robert Shaw. He was promoted to Corporal while still in basic training. Charles and Louis Douglass, the son's of Frederick Douglass were also in the unit.

During a battle in Savannah, the unit saw a young Mulatto boy running down the street half-naked and screaming. His name was Samuel Ruth, and the thirteen year old, was running for his life. When he saw the Soldiers Samuel panicked, thinking the black soldiers would kill him. As a Mulatto in Savannah Georgia, he was treated badly by slaves and whites. The soldiers convinced the young boy they were there to protect him.

Samuel was taken in by the unit, and served as a personal servant to Sergeant Swails. Samuel Walter Pinn, and the young boy struck up a friendship, and he arranged for the young boy to live with his parents in Burlington New Jersey. The 54th Massachusetts camped out at the Pinn Family home when dropping Samuel off. He remained in that household until the age of twenty-one, when he moved to Chester County Pennsylvania. Maria Pinn, also moved to Chester County, and the couple married in 1871, when they were twenty-one years old.

RECRUITS FOR THE 54ᵀᴴ MASS VOLUNTEERS-COLUMBIA PENNSYLVANIA

"On last Tuesday afternoon our town was the scene of more excitement than it has witnessed since the memorable departure of the bold militia for Harrisburg last fall. A large crowd collected about Blacks, to witness the departure, by the Harrisburg Accommodation East, of the first squad of Colored Volunteers that Columbia has sent to the wars.

The men were recruited here by an agent for the 54ᵗʰ Massachusetts Colored Volunteers, and left here for the East, where they are to be mustered in equipped and paid their bounty of $100 each. The squad consisted of eighteen young men- the first installment only some four others were obtained by sickness, and a number have expressed a determination to enlist. Massachusetts having taken the imitative in the enlistment of Negroes is now reaping the benefit of her policy; her quota is being filled by volunteers from other states. This regiment will probably soon be filled, and others will follow.

We see no reason why Pennsylvania should not offer the same inducements to colored men. Those who have the grit to volunteer in the face of all the difficulties thrown in their way will make good soldiers and we can see no sufficient reason against employing them. As for the idea that the vilest and most degraded Negro is not good enough to shoot a rebel, it is absurd. However, the men who left Columbia were good material and men whose labor will be missed in the spring, when the lumber season opens. We wish them the success and safety that their commendable spirit deserves."[29]

We place their names on the record:
- John Anderson
- Sylvester Burrell
- Elijah Berry
- Robert Cain
- James Davis
- Charles Elder

Henry Parker
*Samuel (Walter) Pinn
George Prosser
Warner Ryan
John Stotts
William Thompson

- William Edgely   Benjamin Thompson
- James Jackson   John J. Turner
- William Kelley   Edward Parker

*The preceding list holds the names of the soldiers who served from Lancaster County Pennsylvania. Great Uncle, Samuel Walter Pinn, was barely five feet tall, with brown hair, fair skin, and light eyes. The Unit was depicted in the movie "Glory," as heroes, and deservedly so. He and the 54th Massachusetts United States Colored Troops fought the good fight, putting their lives on the line for freedom. In a country that treated them as if they were strangers, and they were, "A Cut Above."

⌘ ⌘ ⌘

CHAPTER SEVEN

⚯ ⚯

LEAVING THEIR MARK
OUR RUTH FAMILY

Research requires access to resources, whether through the internet, by letter or in person. Make time to do thorough research, and be prepared to ask questions. Let the person you are communicating with know, who, what, and where. If the information is there, those three questions can get you to it. If you are easily frustrated, do not even bother it is better to pay someone else to do it. While researching your Multi-Racial Ancestors, it is important to retain objectivity. This is especially true for those who are researching Native and African Ancestry.

The first document I obtained was the military records for my ancestors, Uriah Martin and Henry Green. There was a wealth of information contained in those documents, much of which supported my mother's stories. Both were in the 41st United States Colored Troops (USCT), out of Lancaster County Pennsylvania.

As stated earlier, my mother was our family historian, and gave details that became important in later research. For instance, she said that, our ancestors Uriah Martin Tamyzine Page, and Henry Green had Native Ancestry. For a while, it seemed like I was looking for a needle in a haystack, because of the racial laws. She also stated that the Martin and Page family were in Pennsylvania prior to the time of William Penn. She also said that they knew the area of Pennsylvania like the back of their hands.

THE WARNER AND RUTH STORIES

Mom was the keeper of our family history, and often shared stories with us. We were her captive audience, especially during the cold winter months. In the winter, we sat around our pot-bellied stove and listened to her stories about the ancestors, and their exploits. One of the story she was how our ancestor, Great-Great Grandmother Warner handled her light skinned grandchildren. Mom said that she was born in Guinea West Africa, and sold as a slave when she was twelve. She was the mother of Great-Grandfather, Samuel Ruth the son of the white man who owned her, Robert Ruth.

After her husband Jack Warner and son George passed away, Grandmother Leah Warner lived on land owned by her son Samuel Ruth. When she arrived from South Carolina, her light-skinned Grandchildren made comments about how black she was. One of the children pointed at her and said, "Who is that Black woman?" Leah grabbed the child and began beating him, before she was stopped. From that point on, her son, Samuel Ruth told his mother to let him discipline the children. As a slave, she endured taunts from whites, and even other slaves, and would not tolerate disrespect from her Grandchildren. She got the respect of her grandchildren, all of whom spoke lovingly of their Grandmother Warner.

Great Grandmother Leah, like many other slaves felt the sting of the whip across her back on many occasions. Each morning as they went into the fields, the overseer Mr. Fields, rode in on his horse with his whip cracking. They would run hard and fast, but those in the back felt heard the crack and felt the sting of the whip. On many occasions, the whip found its mark on Leah's back. The wounds were left to fester under the hot sun, as they worked in the fields.

After the Civil War, Mr. Fields continued to whip the now freed slaves. Leah asked if he was still allowed to whip them, since they were no longer slaves. She was told that he was no longer allowed to whip her or the others. The next morning as they headed into the field, the overseer rode out on his horse, with whip in hand. Leah slowed down and let him raise the whip, before she grabbed it, and yanked him off his horse. She proceeded to whip him until he was near death. He heard the crack of the whip, the same sound the slaves had heard, over the years. It must have felt like sweet justice to Leah, as she whipped him nearly to death. She may have intended to kill the overseer, but her husband intervened and pulled her away. That was the last time they saw Mr. Fields, or his whip.

During her enslavement and after having children by her white owner, Leah was given permission to marry another slave. His name was Jack Warner and their marriage lasted until his death around 1880. Prior to her marriage to Mr. Warner, she had children, Emily, Samuel, Daniel, and Isabella Ruth, by the white man who owned her. In 1857, she and the children were sold from the Ruth Plantation in Beaufort District South Carolina, to what is now Hilton Head South Carolina. Her Mulatto children were sold to Savannah Georgia.

In the 1870, Federal Census Leah is living with her husband, Jack Warner, daughter Isabella who was fifteen, and George who was eleven. In the 1880 Federal Census, Leah is listed as living by herself still in Hilton Head, and is listed as a widow. She would later state that her husband, Mr. Warner, had passed away, and that, "they killed Georgy." We do not know who, "they" were, or why they killed Georgy. By then Isabella was living in Savannah, where she eventually married. She was still living there in 1938, when, Samuel Ruth passed.

There are discrepancies in the census records regarding her age and place of birth. In the Beaufort District 1870 Federal Census for South Carolina, Leah's age is listed as thirty-seven years old. In the 1870 and 1880 census for Hilton Head South Carolina, her birthplace is South Carolina. Her birthplace is listed as Georgia in the 1910 Federal Census for East Fallow field, Chester County Pennsylvania. In the 1910 Federal Census for Chester County Pennsylvania, her age is listed as one hundred. That means she was born about 1812, closer to the birth date in her stories. My guess is that the first two census takers were guessing her age, and where she was born.

The 1880 Federal Census for Georgia lists the white father of Leah Warner's children, Robert Ruth, as living in Effingham

County Georgia with his wife Mary, and son Levi. In the 1850 census Robert, Mary and son Levy are listed as living in Beaufort District South Carolina, St. Peters Parish. In the 1850 Federal Census for Beaufort District South Carolina, Robert Ruth lists his occupation as planter, but only had five slaves. However, he could have had the use of other slaves to plant and grow cotton.

The country Leah was enslaved from was, Guinea West Africa, and her tribe was the Malinke. They were Muslims who came into Guinea from Mali, and are descendants of the rulers at Timbuktu and were ruled by the Keita and Camary families. The Malinke Tribe, entered Guinea from around 1350 AD, and ruled over the Baga, the indigenous people of Guinea. They also brought the Muslim Religion to the area, and many wars were fought between the Baga and Malinke.

Leah survived the Middle Passage, and all of the horrors of slavery. She was more powerful then all of those who set out to take her freedom. There is one picture of her, taken about 1912, and sitting on the porch of her house in Erculdon Pennsylvania. She is looking right in the camera, with her hands crossed, a white dress, and a black shawl covering her head. She appears to have a Muslim Wrap with the scarf draped and wrapped around her head. She was about ninety-seven years old then, having lived longer than those who enslaved her.

In the 1880 Federal Census for the Chatham District of Savannah, Daniel Ruth,, Leah Warner's son is attending school, and her daughter Emily Ruth is living in the Dillon Household in Savannah Georgia. He is attending school, and Emily is a Housekeeper, in the Dillon Household. David and Rachel Dillon (husband and Wife), are listed as the Dillion's children. David Dillon, a banker, is the Head of Household, and his worth is listed as five hundred thousands dollars. One of his children is attending school in Europe, and he has assets well over three-hundred thousand dollars, (a millionaire by today's standards).

In the 1900 Federal Census for Georgia, Daniel Ruth was living in Ocilla Town Georgia, with his wife and children. He lists his occupation as Teamster, his race as black, and appears to be doing well. I do not see a listing for Emily after 1870, possibly because she was married. After the Civil War, Leah's Children, seem to have done well for themselves, especially Samuel Ruth, who was an Elder at the Church of Christ, and a prominent farmer in Pennsylvania.

Chester Ruth, the son of Samuel and Louisa Ruth's son was an Inventor, and owned his own Machine Shop in Coatesville. Ida E. Ruth-Jones, their daughter is a well-respected Folk Artist in Pennsylvania. Chester Ruth and Ida E. Ruth-Jones have plaques erected in their honor, in Chester and Lancaster County. Another son, Walter Ruth was a musician for President Warren Harding, in Washington DC.

THE RUTH'S OF PENNSYLVANIA

Samuel Ruth's Obituary in 1938, stated that he was a prominent, "Colored" farmer in Chester County. He was no longer that slave boy, who ran through the streets of Savannah Georgia, screaming and crying. Samuel and Maria Pinn-Ruth were people of faith, who dediciated their lives to God, Family, and Community. Two of the children, William Chester Ruth, and Ida Ella Ruth-Jones, made extraordinary contributions.

William Chester Ruth was an inventor, who opened a blacksmith and Machine Shop in 1923. He was also a father and and elder at the Church of Christ Erculdon. Great Grandfather Samuel Ruth, was also an inventor, but he did not know about patents. Chester Ruth learned how to patent his inventions, after one of his inventions was stolen, and patented.

WILLIAM CHESTER RUTH 1882–1971

African American inventor who opened a blacksmith and machine shop (on Lincoln Highway) here in 1923. He did metal work and repairs, primarily for Pennsylvania German farmers. Ruth designed and patented many agricultural devices, most notably his 1928 baler feeder. He also applied his talents to designing and building military devices. An esteemed community member, he was spiritual leader at the Church of Christ in Ercildoun, where he lived.

He was an inventor who had at least fifty-two patents. As a child, he had an uncontrollable urge to take his toys apart. This inquisitive nature led him to invent numerous pieces of farm equipment and machinery. He moved from Ercildoun, Pennsylvania to Gap Pennsylvania in 1917. Great Uncle Chester Ruth worked for Luken's Steel Mill when he moved to Gap. In 1923, he opened Ruth's Ironworks Shop. His descendants continue to live in Lancaster and Chester County. During World War II, the US government commissioned William Chester Ruth to design and manufacture secret devices for airplanes and bomb sightings. He was the first person in our family who owned his own Manufacturing Business.

Some of his inventions were:
- The Baler-feeder
- The Automatic Tie Baler
- The Manure Spreader
- Part for Trident Missle
- The adaptor for the grain elevator
- Part for light bulb, which enabled it to be plugged into a light socket
- The Cinder spreader

IDA ELLA RUTH-JONES ARTIST

Great Aunt Ida Jones spent her life raising a family, and active in the Church of Christ at Erculdon. She was married to William O. Jones, who was a Blacksmith, and Elder at the Church. Once her children were raised, and after her husband passed, Aunt Ida started painting. Her paintings were discovered by Horace Mann-Bond, the President of Lincoln University. She painted over three hundred painting in her seventies and eighties.

IDA ELLA RUTH-JONES (1874–1959)

African American self-taught artist who depicted life in rural Chester County in the first half of the 20th century. The daughter of a former slave, Jones completed more than 300 works in her 70s and 80s. She worked in watercolor, oil, and pencil in a style typical of folk art. Her works illustrated personal observations of family and farm life, nature, landscapes, early technologies, human interaction, and slavery. Jones resided on a nearby farm.

Ida E. Ruth-Jones, is my Grandmother, Leah Ruth-Martin's older sister. Her descendants continue to live in and around Coatesville Pennsylvania. One of her daughters, Ida Jones-Williams, is an author and educator in Virginia. Cousin Ida J. Williams has written several books, including a book about Great-Great Grandmother Leah Ruth-Warner. Ida's Great Granddaughter, Vanessa Julye is a Quaker Missionary, and is a writer, photographer, and Author.

GULLAH CULTURE AND GREAT-GREAT GRANDMOTHER LEAH WARNER

The Plantation System in South Carolina was similar to the one in the Caribbean. Slaves formed their own communities, under the watchful eye of an overseer, whose only concern was what they could produce. Some of the Islands off of the South Carolina Coast continue to house the Gullah People, who were former slaves. They have a vibrant culture that continues to thrive, and each year they hold a festival. In the Upper South, the slaves usually lived on a Plantation, under the watchful eye of their Master. Many of the Island Slaves were owned by large corporations, which hired and fired overseers. In both systems, the slaves were subjected to emotional and/or physical control to secure the desired economic results.

The Gullah are descendants of African Slaves, who live in the Low Country of South Carolina, which includes both the coastal plain and the Sea Islands. The Gullah Region once extended north to the Cape Fear area on the coast of North Carolina and south to the vicinity of Jacksonville on the coast of Florida. Today the Gullah area is confined to the South Carolina and Georgia Sea Islands Country. The Geechie were slaves imported from West Africa as rice growers, and lived along the Ogeechie River in South Carolina's Low Country.

Gullah-Geechie is a language and a culture derived from slaves in the low lands of Georgia and South Carolina. slaves, are known for preserving their African linguistic and cultural heritage. They speak an English-based Creole language containing many African words and significant influences from African languages in grammar and sentence structure. The Gullah Language is similar to Jamaican Creole, Bahamian Dialect, and the Krio (Creole) language of Sierra Leone in West Africa. Gullah storytelling,food, music, folk beliefs, crafts, farming and fishing traditions.

Great-Great Grandmother Leah Warner, found comfort when she was sold to Hilton Head (Hog) Island. She moved from a small farm where there were only five other slaves, to an island with a sea of black faces. Living there gave her a semblance of a life with her husband Jack, and their remaining children. The physical labor helped to keep her mind off of her babies, who were sold to Savannah Georgia. She remained there until after the death of her husband, when her son Sammy, took her to Pennsylvania. Although it was the deep south, Pennsylvania was not the haven it appeared to be on the surface.

There were incidents in Pennsylvania which were just as horrific as events in South Carolina. One was the lynching of Zachariah Walker, a black man, who was accused of murdering a white man.

A PENNSYLVANIA LYNCHING – ZACHARIAH WALKER

My mother often told the story of Zachariah Walker, who was lynched in Coatesville. The murder took place in 1911, years before my mother was born. But it was only a year before Great-Grandmother Leah Ruth died, and what must she have thought. When my mother told the story, it was as if she had witnessed the event. She stated that Walker was involved with the wife of Rice, (a Policeman). When Rice found out about it, his wife claimed that she had been raped. This is not the version that is reported in the Newspaper, it is the back-story.

There were other members of the community, who told the same version of events. That is not the popular or acceptable version, it is another version. After the death of Rice, when he was being hunted by the white mob, Zachariah attempted suicide, and was taken to the local hospital. He was dragged out of the hospital still shackled to the bed, by the white mob. They dragged him to a field where he was beaten and set on fire. There were hundreds of onlookers many of whom were women and children. After the fire cooled down, some of the on lookers cut pieces of his body off for souvenirs.

One of the members of the mob was a candidate for Governor, who cheered the crowd on. This was not South Carolina, Mississippi, or Louisiana, it was Chester County Pennsylvania. This northern county, was not more than twenty miles from where, in 1765, the last Indian Massacre took place. No one was convicted of the murder of Zachariah Walker. In fact, when he staggered from the pyre, a mass of flames, they shoved him back in. Men, women, and children, stood for photographs alongside of the body with ghoulish smiles on their faces. My mother said that Coatesville was taken off the maps, after this incident. She also stated that no plants or trees would grow on the site where Zachariah Walker was tortured and burned to death.

Following is an article written by John Jay Chapman (in 1912) ; about the death of Zachariah Walker:
"The subject we are dealing with is not local. The act, to be sure, took place at Coatesville and everyone looked to Coatesville to follow it up. Some months ago, I asked a friend who lives not far from here something about this case, and about the expected prosecutions and he replied to me: "It wasn't in my county," and that made me wonder whose county it was in. And it seemed to be in my county. I live on the Hudson River; but I knew that the great wickedness that happened in Coatesville is not the wickedness of Coatesville nor of today. It is the wickedness of all America and of three hundred years — the wickedness of the slave trade. All of us are tinctured by it. No special place, no special persons, are to blame...'
The subject we are dealing with is not local. The act, to be sure, took place at Coatesville and everyone looked to Coatesville to follow it up. Some months ago, I asked a friend who lives not far from here something about this case, and about the expected prosecutions and he replied to me: "It wasn't in my county," and that made me wonder whose county it was in; and it seemed to be in my county. I live on the Hudson River; but I knew that the great wickedness that happened in Coatesville is not the wickedness of Coatesville nor of today. It is the wickedness of all America and of three hundred years — the wickedness of the slave trade. All of us are tinctured by it."[30]

⌘ ⌘ ⌘

CHAPTER EIGHT

⚡ ⚡

FFV- THE FIRST FAMILIES OF VIRGINIA

The real First Families of Virginia (FFV) were not from England and did not speak with a British accent. The very first human residents in Virginia probably walked here from Asia through Alaska, after crossing the Bering Land Bridge. There is a small chance that the first Virginians sailed here from the Solute region of France about 15,000 years ago, but the first Virginians certainly did not arrive in the Susan, Constant, Godspeed, and Discovery in 1607.[31]

The Virginia Company of London, "discovered," the land known as Virginia, after the Jamestown landing in 1607. The discovery of land came complete with a Native population, which had occupied the area for thousands of years. America has only been in existence about four hundred years, and has managed to wipe out thousands of years of Native Culture. There were natives, who believing that the newcomers were friends, assisted Europeans. Many Native People perished from European diseases, and aggression (including enslavement), and forced relocation.

Before the Native issue was resolved, African slaves began arriving in Virginia. It was then that the three racial groups in Colonial Virginia were White, Native, and African. The intermixing of these three groups created other racial classifications of Negro, Colored, and Mulatto. Other racial classifications were used, especially in the deep south, such as Octoroon, Mustee, and Quadroon, prior to the Civil War. Those identifications were used widely used in the Deep South, prior to the Civil War.

Historians often refer to Virginia as the, "Upper South," as if to distance it from the other slave holding states. It also has the distinction of having more Presidents then any other state. The slave ports in Virginia were at primarily at Alexandria, Fredericksburg, and Richmond. My Virginia ancestors were European, Native, and Africans, who intermixed and became Mulatto, or Persons of Color. Most African Americans are mixed raced, and are more of an ethnic group, then a race. Many of the prominent names in Virginia had some connection to my ancestors, including the Washington and Monroe families. The Pinn Indians, intermixed and married Free Blacks (and slaves), in Northumberland and Lancaster County Virginia.

In 1669, when the Pinn Surname was first recorded in Virginia, much of the native way of life had disappeared. The Pinn Indians occupied the Eastern Shore of Virginia and Maryland for thousands of years. Pinn Indians were those who wore a pin on the right lapel to signify they were Christians.[32]

Several European lines, specifically Lewis, Monroe, Bowden, and Hilliard, and Cooper, also intermixed with Natives and Africans. There are other connected lines out of Virginia, which have been more elusive including the Rowe, and Rogers. Unraveling, "Who, What, and Where", was a task complicated by the racial designations separating the groups. Some lines jumped from one designation to another within a generation, and the surnames changed as well.

There is a myth bolstered by some historians that Natives and Blacks did not intermix. The truth is that both groups were lumped together economically, racially, and geographically. They were enslaved, deprived of a land base, and considered, Colored, Negro, or Mulatto. When laws were passed to guarantee Americans their Rights, Indians and blacks were left out. The racial classification of natives who were assimilated was changed to white.

Much of Colonial Virginia's interracial mixing took place on plantations and farms scattered throughout the Colony. Detailed records kept on the slaves and servants, are stored in various repositories including, court documents (e.g. wills), bills of sale, indentures, and tax records. The Church Vestrymen kept records, and policed the church members in each parish. Throughout the parish, church attendance was mandatory, and non-compliance led to fines, sanction, and Jail.

The surviving Vestry Records of the Episcopalian and Anglican Churches reflect church membership and attendance. They are not readily available, as many were returned to England, and others are housed in Library Collections. Parishioners were fined in tobacco, which at the time was worth more then the English Pound. The Episcopalian and Anglican Churches also kept Baptism Record, as well as birth, marriage and death records. These days most of the major churches have Historical Societies and some records on past members.

TOBACCO THE NOXIOUS WEED

Smoking, wrote King James I, in his 1604 "A Counterblast to Tobacco," is "a custom loathsome to the eye, hateful to the nose, harmful to the brain, dangerous to the lungs, and in the black stinking fume thereof, nearest resembling the horrible Stygian smoke of the pit that is bottomless."

Land confiscated from Natives, and redistributed to Europeans, became the Plantations, and farms of Colonial Virginia. The cash crop was not food or cotton, but tobacco, "The Noxious Weed," sold to European Smoke Shops. The African labor and Native lands were used to grow and ship the weed overseas. Slaves were assigned work that was unsuited for whites, such as planting tobacco, constructing buildings, working in Iron Ore Plants, mining, and other physical tasks. The house slaves took care of all household duties, which included cooking, cleaning, childcare, and nursing sick family members back to health. Another task for slaves was working on the Ship Yards loading and unloading cargo, headed into and out of Virginia Ports. Fredericksburg and The Port of Richmond created untold wealth for Virginia's Landed Gentry.

The laws of Colonial Virginia were made by the Planters, and centered on their inalienable right to life, liberty, and the pursuit of happiness. In the eyes of the Colonialists those rights did not include, Natives and any other Persons of Color (Free or Slave). The indentured servants from Europe signed contracts for seven years of labor to pay for their passage. There were other Indentured Servants, e.g., Mulattoes, who served forced indentures (thirty years for females, twenty years for males). Unless slaves had an owner who set them free, they were slaves for life.

THREE GENERATIONS OF WASHINGTON AND MONROE SERVANTS - HILLIARD, MONROE, AND BOWDEN LINES

Lydia Hilliard was the first of three generations of related females, living in the household of William Monroe Senior. In 1706, she was living in Westmoreland County Virginia, facing a charge of Bastardy, for having a child by a Negro man. The child was named Mary (last name unknown), and a subsequent lawsuit followed regarding her custody. At the time, Lydia was a servant in the house of William Monroe (Senior).

The lawsuit was an attempt by William Monroe Senior to regain custody of his servants' child. William Munroe (Monroe) Senior took Reverend St. Shropshire to court to obtain physical custody of the Mulatto child. In the suit, Lydia Hilliard, was identified as a servant and living at the Monroe Household. The court awarded William Monroe Senior custody of the child, and absolved him of payment for her care. By 1730, the child, now named Mary Monroe, was also taken to court on a Charge of Bastardy.

Mary Bowden was born on February 20, 1730, to Mary and William Monroe Junior, (the Uncle of President James Monroe). William Monroe Junior was born about 1710 to William and Margaret Babcock Monroe. It appears that there was a marriage between William Monroe Junior and Mary Monroe, which was not legal. The marriage went against Virginia's law against interracial marriage. In May of 1730, a Grand Jury met in Westmoreland County, with the intention of indicting Mary Monroe for Bastardy. In July of 1730, the Grand Jury threw out the indictment, citing that the law did not allow marriage between Mulatto Women and White Men. In other words, there was a catch-22 situation for the parties involved, thus the case was thrown out.

EXCERPTS FROM WESTMORELAND COUNTY ORDER BOOK 1705–1721

29 MAY 1706

William Munroe (Monroe), by his Petition to this Court showing that the Churchwardens of Washington Parish in the said County bound a certain mulatto child to him according to Law and that the child was now in the custody of the Reverend St.. John Shropshire refused to deliver the child to him, and the said Munro (Monroe), prayed the Court's Order for the said Shropshire's delivery of the child to him.

The said Shropshire, by Daniel McCarty his Attorney, be it humbly moved that in consideration that the mulatto Child was born in his house on the body of one Lydia Hilliard; who is his Servant; and that he had from the time of the birth of the child which is now about the space of two whole years; maintained the child and was ready to give Bond to save the Parish harmless; and indemnified of the child provided it were bound to him as in right he conceives it to be just and equitable and prayed the child may be bound to him according to Law; or otherwise that such Order might be made therein as he might be recompensed by such methods as the Court should think reasonable, that he might deserve for the maintenance of the Child during the time the Child was so maintained.

Upon hearing what was alleged on each part, it is the opinion of the Court that the Indenture by which the Child was bound to said Munro (Monroe) was good and effectual in the Law and order the said Shropshire do forthwith deliver the child to said Munro, &c. St. John Shropshire appealed the decision of the Westmoreland Court to the General Court who apparently returned it with the instructions to look into the matter further, which the Court did by appointing Caleb Butler, Gent; and Joshua Davies to study the matter and make their recommendation, and if they could not agree to appoint a referee which they did, being Lewis Markham, Gent., "not agreeing do make choice of Mr. Lewis Markham, Gent. To decide the same and doe therefore award that St. John Shropshire deliver to William Munro (Monroe) the Mulatto without any recompense for the keeping and nursing of the same.

Lydia Hilliard, born say 1685, was the white woman servant of the Reverend St. John Shropshire on 25 April 1705 when she was convicted by the Westmoreland County Court of having a "mulatto" child by a "Negro man." She was the servant of William Munro (Monroe) Washington Parish on, 8 March 1706, when he complained to the court that he had maintained her "Mulatto" child for two years, and that the Reverend St. John Shropshire refused to release the child to him.[33]

In 1736, a "Mulatto" called Mol (a nickname for Mary), was adjudged, by the Westmoreland County Court, (in Monroe Virginia), to be seven years old, and indentured to Augustine Washington Senior. When the courts indentured Mary Bowden to the Washington's, she was at the household of Thomas Chilton. It is not clear why the Chilton's did not receive the child's Indenture. The trigger for the child's indenture seems to be the death of William Monroe and her mother. The community decided who was what, and it would not take long to get that information to the courts. In court, only certain persons held sway, specifically, "White Anglo Saxon" Males.[34]

Mary Monroe, and William Monroe Junior's marriage, was essentially absolved by the Grand Jury. It is not clear if William Monroe Junior was still alive after 1737, or even in the area. The court documents prove the familial ties between the Monroe and Chilton family, and thus to Mary Monroe. The documents show the familial relationship between Mary Monroe, and Thomas Chilton. Andrew Monroe, the son of William Monroe Senior and his wife Mary Bowcock. Andrew Monroe, the brother of William Monroe Junior, was the father of President James Monroe.[35]

THE BOWDEN'S OF POPES CREEK

Mary Bowden is a direct ancestor, through her daughter, Patty Bowden-Jackson who was born about 1750 at Popes Creek Plantation in Westmoreland County Virginia. The Washington Family Plantation is located along the Potomac River, an easy escape route for those seeking freedom. The Plantation was later called Wakefield, and is now George Washington Birthplace. Patty's father may have been another Mulatto, or a slave on the plantation. While in an indenture, slaves and servants could not marry without permission. There were informal ceremonies, such as Jumping of the Broom, performed within the slave community.

Mary ran away several times while serving her indenture, possibly going down the Potomac. The last attempt was in 1758, when she escaped to Essex County, and remained there for several years. After her capture, she was given more time, and fined for causing her master, Augustine Washington Junior, expenditures to search for her. There were no accounts of Patty running away; not surprising since, Popes Creek was the only home she knew.

Patty's knick name was, "Free Patty," possibly given to her by the slaves. She may have had a relationship with her father, if he was a slave at Popes Creek. It is doubtful that Mary was in charge of raising Patty, because of her tendency to run away. The raising of her child would have been assigned to trusted servant in the household. She may have been under the most trusted servant in the household, who taught her charge well. Patty was given the trusted position of personal servant to Augustine Washington Juniors' daughter Elizabeth.

The question of Patty's father may lay in a slave graveyard at George Washington Birthplace. It is located in the woods on the property of a Washington descendant, next to George Washington Birthplace. The bodies were sat in the grave, without caskets or covering, and no consecration. It is just a place out in the woods among tall trees, off the side of a path. I visited the grave one time in October of 1999, and was saddened to see how the area is treated. The area is surrounded by trees, in contrast to the Graves on at George Washington Birthplace. It is as if these souls are still enslaved, and have no freedom even in death. The owner, who is a descendent of the Washington's, has not granted further access to the graves.

Virginia's trespassing laws, prevents access to graveyards on private property, without the owner's permission. Even in death, the slaves are not free, but continue to be under the authority of those who enslaved them. It would be a simple matter for the authorities to allow access to common graveyards in Virginia, through easements. That would allow those of us, who have relatives buried in the Commonwealth to visit their graves.

When Mary escaped, in 1752, she left Patty at Popes Creek, possibly knowing that she would face severe penalties for taking the child. She most certainly would have been charged with stealing personal property, no different from being a Horse Thief. The penalty for stealing her child (theft), ranged from a fine, to jail time, to whipping, and in some cases hanging. In one of her escape attempts she was found living with a man named Sibbald, who Augustine Washington attempted to prosecute. The case was eventually dismissed after all there was no credible evidence to convict him.

Mary Bowden was a Mulatto Woman, and a run away someone whose testimony had no weight in court. Mary's frequent attempts to live free were met with the heavy hand of the law, which increased her servitude to nearly forty years. Yet, she lived quite a bit of her life in freedom, and was alive and well in 1810, living in Fredericksburg. It is doubtful that Mary received a glowing reference after her indenture ended, and she left the Washington Household.

FREE IN FREDERICKSBURG- BOWDEN LEWIS JACKSON

After completing her indenture, Patty moved to Fredericksburg, and resided on the property of Charles Yates. Alexander Spotswood wrote a recommendation praising Patty Bowden for her excellent service. While a servant, she bore at least two children, Anne Webb, and Delphi. Although her daughter, Anne Webb remained in servitude, Delphi was released to Patty by Alexander Spotswood, "for her faithful service."

Anne Webb's indenture was purchased by her husband, Aminidab Booker after the death of Charles Yates. Patty (Martha) Bowden-Jackson is identified in the Fredericksburg Free Negro Registry (1830), as a dark mulatto, five feet, four inches tall. Her future husband James Jackson, was a house servant to Charles Yates, and lived in his house.

Sylvia, the mother of, James Jackson, was a trusted house servant to Charles Yates, before her death. Yates mentions that Sylvia was the mother of James Jackson, in tax documents he filed with the City of Fredericksburg. Patty and James Jackson had children, James Junior, Samuel, William, and Leroy, prior to their marriage. However they may have had a marriage ceremony, and been recognized as husband and wife.

While living in the Servants Quarters of Yates property, Patty worked as a tailor. James Jackson and all of the servants in Yates household were freed by his will. Yates owned at least one other plantation where slaves worked the fields, and they were not freed. There is not a lot of available information on James Jackson. He was deceased before 1810 when Patty is listed as paying taxes on their home.

Another trusted servant mentioned by Yates was Aminidab Booker, who came to Virginia from London England. He was an indentured servant to a Mr. Homer, who sent a letter praising him to Charles Yates. In the letter, he stated that Aminidab was to be freed, and paid wages at the end of his indenture. Upon Charles Yates death, he left five hundred dollars to Aminidab Booker. Once Aminidab was free, he changed his last name to Jackson, and then married Patty's daughter, Anne Webb.

In a move that proved his love and affection, he purchased Anne Webb's Indenture, before they married. They had several children, Patty Junior, James, Samuel, and William, all with the last name of Jackson. Mary and Patty Bowden both lived well into their eighties near the Rappahannock River in Fredericksburg. Patty worked as a tailor, and purchased a property on Princess Ann Street with James and their children.

Samuel Jackson (the son of James and Patty Bowden-Jackson) married another Free Mulatto, Maria Lewis, about 1822 in

Fredericksburg. She is my ancestor, through Nancy Lewis; and was born about 1800, to Nancy, and an unknown male. Maria is described as a mulatto about five feet four inches tall, in the 1822 Free Negro Registry for Fredericksburg. Her mother, Nancy Lewis, was the daughter of Charles and Susannah Lewis, and was born in Richmond Virginia. There is no menton of Maria's father, who may have been a slave or Indentured Servant, and not free to marry.

Maria and Samuel Jackson were the parents of Elizabeth Jackson, Anne Jackson, and Walter Jackson. Maria died young, sometime before 1838, when her daughter Elizabeth married. Nancy Lewis took over the raising of her grandchildren, after the death of their parents. Samuel Jackson died shortly after his mother (Patty Bowden), and willed the family home to his three children. In 1838 Elizabeth Jackson, Samuel and Maria's daughter, married Robert A. Pinn. He was a Baptist minister from Amherst County Virginia. Most of the socializing between Free Blacks was through the Church, and in Fredericksburg, it was the Baptist Church.

DOCUMENTATION AND RECORDS FROM WESTMORELAND COUNTY VIRGINIA

July 1730, p.341

Grand Jury vs. Mary Munroe (Monroe) Mulatto Woman; Ordered that the Sheriff of this County do summon Mary a Mulatto servant woman belonging to Wm Munroe, of the Parish of Washington to be (dark film?)., Bastard child born of her body (very dark film)

27 August 1730, p.338

Mary a Mulatto Servant to William Monroe of Washington Parish being presented by the grand jury at May Court last for having a bastard child on or about the 20th of February last past which being now Called and the Court taking the Same under Consideration they are of opinion that Mulatto Women are Not within the penalty of the Law Against Bastardy they being by the Law of the Country prohibited marriage with White Men, And therefore It is ordered that the presentment be Dismist.

3 April 1737, proved 26 April 1737

Granddaughter Elizabeth Sanford; Capt. Andrew Munroe and his wife Jane to have care of her estate until she is 18 years of age; son John Watts; son James Bowcock and his children Thomas, James, and Jane; son Richard Watts; daughters Jane Munroe, Margaret Strother, and Mary Blackburn and the latter's husband Mr. Richard Blackburn; Capt. Thomas Chilton and his wife Jemima 1 mourning ring each; Rev. Roderick McCullough a Mourning Ring.

26 March 1751, p.31

It is Ordered that the Churchwardens of Washington Parish do bind Martha (Patty) Bowden a Mulatto Child of Mary Bowden to Augustine Washington, Gent. according to Law.

21 February 1752, p.109

Robert Sibbald being bound over to this Court by John Elliott upon the Complaint of Augustine Washington Gent., for detaining a Mulatto Woman (Mary Bowden); of the said Washington upon hearing the Complaint of the said Washington, and the Examination of Several Witnesses the Court are of Opinion that the said Sibbald ought not to be bound to his good behavior, therefore do order that he be discharged from his recognizance.

26 May 1752, p.124

Augustine Washington Gent. bringing before this Court his Mulatto Servant Woman named Mary Bowden, for Absenting herself from her Master's Service Five Months, and he making Oath that he hath Expended One hundred and Eighty Pounds of Tobacco in taking her up, & the said Mary having nothing to say in her own defense, It is therefore Ordered that she do serve her said Master his heirs & Assigns, after her time by Indenture is Expired, One Year two Weeks & five days for said Absent time & Expenses.

Westmoreland County Orders 1758–1761

29 August 1758, P.1a

Mary Bowden a Mulatto Servant was brought to face the Court & Ordered to serve her Master Augustine Washington

Gent. His heirs and assigns Four Years & Six Months. The time served for two years runaway time & fees (?) To be expended after her indentured time is expired.

26 June 1706, p.27a to 28

William Munro (e) by his Petition to this Court showing that the Churchwardens of Washington Parish in the said county had bound a certain Mulatto bastard child to him according to Law and that the said child was now in the custody of the Reverend St. John Shropshire who refused to deliver the child to him the said Munro; and prayed the Court order for the said Shropshires delivery of the said Child to him.

The said Shropshire by Daniel McCarty his attorney humbly moves that in consideration the said Mulatto child was born in his house on the body of one Lydia Hilliard his servant and that he had from the time of the birth of said child which is now above the space of two whole years maintained the said child and was ready to give bond to save the parish harmless and indemnified of the said child provided it were bound to him as in right he conceives it to bee just & equitable and prayed the said child might be bound to him according to Law. (Ordered that) indenture by which the said child was bound to the said Munro was good and effectual in Law.

26 June 1706, p.27a to 28

Arbitration between Shropshire and Munro, said St. John Shropshire deliver unto the said Wm Munro the said Mulatto without any recompense for the keeping or nursing the Same Given under our hands this twenty Sixth day of June 1706.[36]

TEN GENERATIONS – Lineage – Anita Baxter-Wills to Lydia Hilliard of Westmoreland County Virginia

Generation 1- Wills, Anita Baxter ,

Generation 2-daughter of Baxter, Vivian-Martin (born 1923, Chester County Pennsylvania);

Generation 3-daughter of Martin, Leah-Ruth (b. abt. 1884, Chester County Pennsylvania);

Generation 4-daughter of Ruth, Maria Louisa-Pinn (b. abt. 1850, Fredericksburg Virginia);

Generation 5-daughter of Pinn, Elizabeth-Jackson; (b. abt. 1822, Fredericksburg Virginia)

Generation 6-daughter of Jackson, Samuel (b. abt. 1820, Fredericksburg Virginia)

Generation 7-son of Jackson, Patty-Bowden (b. 1750, Westmoreland County Virginia);

Generation 8- daughter of Bowden, Mary (b. Feb 20, 1730, Westmoreland County Virginia);

Generation 9-daughter of Monroe, Mary (b. abt, 1706, Westmoreland County Virginia);

Generation 10-daughter of Hilliard, Lydia (b. abt. 1690, Westmoreland County Virginia)

⌘ ⌘ ⌘

CHAPTER NINE

≈ ≈

DNA OUT OF AFRICA SEVEN DAUGHTERS OF EVE

According to Family Tree DNA, "All mtDNA lineages trace back to a common ancestor who lived in Africa 100,000 to 150,000 years ago." Some of the lines migrated Out of Africa about 60,000 years ago, while others remained. Lineages that historically remained in Africa include Haplogroup, L1, L2, L3, and M1. Lineages that historically migrated Out of Africa descend from the other Haplogroup.[37]

A Low-Resolution Match occurs when two individuals have exactly the same sequence in the HVR1. As long as they are in the same Haplogroup, these two individuals very likely share a common ancestor at some point on the maternal line. A Low-Resolution Match has about a fifty percent chance of sharing a common ancestor within the last fifty-two generations (about 1300 years). If the Haplogroup, are different, and then the match is coincidental due to "Convergent Evolution", (two unrelated lineages mutate so that they look alike) and there is no common ancestor in thousands or a few tens of thousands of years.

A High-Resolution Match occurs when two individuals have exactly the same sequence in both the HVR1 and HVR2. High-Resolution Matches are the ones, which are more likely to be related within a genealogical period. A High-Resolution

Match has about a fifty percent chance of sharing a Common Ancestor within the last twenty-eight generations (about seven hundred years).

Because mtDNA is passed down from the mother intact in each generation, the answer is that the test can cover both recent and distant generations. On the recent side, the mtDNA Ancestral Origins section will point towards possible countries of origin for the recent ancestors.

The mtDNA test also identifies the Haplogroup, which represents your deep ancestral origins (think tens of thousands of years ago). A Low-Resolution Match means that you have about a fifty percent chance of sharing a common ancestor within the last fifty two generations (about thirteen hundred years), and a High-Resolution Match reduces the figure to around twenty eight generations (about seven hundred years)."

This is about as much as I know about DNA, but there is plenty of information out there. There is the National Geographic Genographics , Family Tree DNA, and Howard University's African Ancestry lab. There are many others but these are some of the more reputable. There are labs that are not reputable, and it would be wise to check before submitting your information. Also on the Family Tree DNA site are DNA Cousins from all over the world. Those who choose too can add their names and email addresses. Some of the DNA Cousin who showed up was people who were already proven through previous research.

The males are at a slight advantage as they have xy Chromosomes, while females have xx chromosomes. The xy chromosomes means the males have a female and male chromosome, and can be tested for male and female DNA. My brother took his first test with Howard University's African Ancestry Lab. He then broadened his results and had his results listed on Family Tree DNA, and showed up as my DNA Cousin. It is exciting to go back eight and nine generations, but putting a face on them was priceless. My female line parallels Charles Lewis our ancestor, whose forbearer,

John Lewis, left Breconshire Wales, around 1650 and settled in Gloucester County Virginia.

The results took us even further down the line in our genetic search, all of the way back to North Africa. Our female ancestor crossed over the Iberian Peninsula about 45,000 years ago. Our mtDNA Haplogroup is T2 (Tara), and that line left North Africa about 45,000 years ago. The clan, or tribe she was with traversed the Iberian Peninsula and settled in what is now the Basque Region of Spain.

Eventually they branched out, and traversed Europe settling in what is now Britain (Wales), around 259 AD. The tribe of my female ancestors was the settlers of Britain, in what is now known as Wales. They remained there through the arrival of the Anglos and Normans, who settled what now England (Anglo) is. Through numerous battles, and intermarriages with Royal Families, the Anglos, conquered Wales, and took possession of the British Isles.

The racial percentages of my mtDNA results, is 87% European, 8% Native, and 5% African. Of course there are other lines, combining within my genes, which create a unique genetic makeup. This line was proved through the mtDNA test (Mitochondria) taken through Family Tree DNA, and connects to Elizabeth of York, the mother of Henry VIII. They were the line of the Tudors, who were conquered by and intermixed with the Stewards; the lines are intermixed with the Welsh and English Royal Family. The male LLewelyn Line is Welsh and is the Lewis (Llewellyn's), of Monmouthshire and Breconshire Wales.

The Paternal line DNA test of my brother proved our Baxter lines to be Native, from Columbia South America Our Paternal Aunt; Ada Baxter-McCracken took a mtDNA Test, which showed the origins of Grandmother Annie Bonaparte-Baxter. Her maternal line is from Northern Nigeria, and part of the Fulani Tribe. Members of this tribe were sold as slaves to the Caribbean, and Puerto Rico.

THE LEWIS LINES FROM EUROPE THROUGH VIRGINIA

My female Lewis lines connects Charles's wife, who was called Hannah (Susannah) Lewis. This line connects to Elizabeth of York, the mother of Henry VIII. They are the Royal family of Wales who were intermixed with England's Royal Family. In my case, DNA and genealogy helped prove a line that is thousands of years old. In Virginia, the female Lewis line is through Colonel John Lewis who was born on 30 Nov 1669. He married Elizabeth Warner, daughter of Col. Augustine Warner II and Mildred Reade, circa 1691. He died on 14 Nov 1725 at 'Warner Hall', Gloucester Co., VA, at age 55. He and Elizabeth Warner resided at 'Warner Hall', Gloucester Co., VA.

Their daughter Elizabeth Lewis is my direct ancestor, (she was baptized on 7 May 1706). She first married William Rush on 12 Jun 1728; and then married Maj. John Bolling, son of Col. John Bolling and Mary Kennon, (the Virginia Bollings show up as DNA cousins on my female line).[38]

The Virginia male Lewis line, begins with John Lewis the planter, who was the father of Zachary Lewis. John Lewis, The Planter, was born in Breconshire Wales, and settled in Gloucester County Virginia, around 1650. His son, Zachary's Lewis, settled in Spotsylvania County with his wife, Betty (Smith), and was the father of John Lewis II. John and Betty Smith-Lewis were the Grandparents of my ancestor, Charles Lewis.

Baxter, George A. (Dad), receiving
Good Conduct Medal circa 1945, Veteran's Hospital
Coatesville Pennsylvania

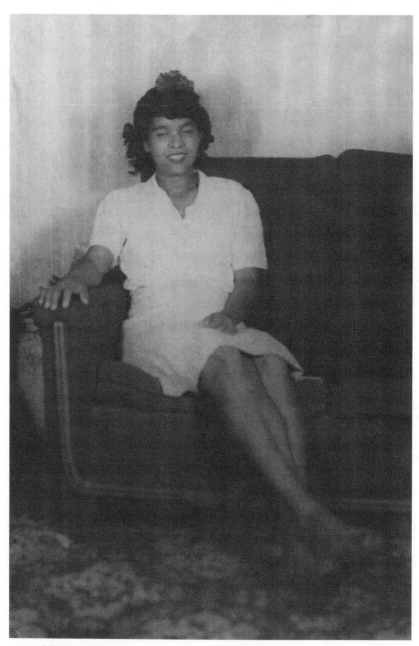

Baxter, Vivian Martin (Mom) – circa 1958
Coatesville Pennsylvania

bottom - Members of Church of Christ Erculdon Pennsylvania circa 1927 - Great Grandfather Samuel Ruth 2nd from right In back row, next to him Great Uncle Chester Ruth.& wife Bertie, Front row 3rd from left is Owen Jones & Ida Ruth-Jones, his wife. Ruth Family home is in the background.

**Grandmother Leah Ruth – Martin circa 1950
Coatesville Pennsylvania**

Baxter, Annie Bonaparte, Charles Wesley
Circa 1920 Orangeburg South Carolina

Pinn, Reverend Robert A. circa 1884
Philadelphia Pennsylvania

Warner, Leah Ruth circa 1912, Erculdon Pennsylvania

**Ruth, William Chester (Great Uncle) Pictured in Ebony Magazine
October 1950 Lancaster County Pennsylvania**

⌘ ⌘ ⌘

CHAPTER TEN

✗ ✗

AMBROSE AND CHARLES LEWIS
REVOLUTIONARY BROTHERS

"Once let the black man get upon his person the brass letter,
U.S., let him get an eagle on his button, and a musket on his
shoulder and bullets in his pocket, there is no power on earth
that can deny that he has earned the right to citizenship."
Frederick Douglasss

The clues for Charles and Ambrose were lying in plain site,
and finally the pieces fell into place. I spent years of research on
Ambrose Lewis, believing that he was my direct ancestor. My interest
was peaked when I found a partial file on him, at the Daughter's of
the American Revolution library. The files proved that Ambrose
served in the Revolutionary War, out of Fredericksburg Virginia.
They brothers were not only Seamen, but also Soldiers, and fought
in the Battle of Camden, South Carolina.

The file gave concrete proof of Ambrose Lewis, age, race,
military service, and place of residence. With this information in
hand, I was able to request specific information on Ambrose Lewis
and find his family. After researching Ambrose for several years,
the clues pointed away from him, and to his brother Charles. Nancy
Lewis, my direct ancestor was the direct connection to Charles and
away from Ambrose. Charles and Ambrose Lewis are believed to
be the sons of a white father (John Lewis), and a Mulatto woman,
(Josephine).

John Lewis was the son of Zachary and Betty-Smith Lewis of Spotsylvania County. There is little background information on the mother, except her first name. Charles was probably the older of the two, born about 1756, while Ambrose was born about 1758. In 1771, the King George County Courts sentenced them to serve twenty-year indentures, under a Mr. Buckingham. The records identified them as Mulatto, "bastards," not surprising since the law did not allow marriages between the races.

As part of their indenture, they were assigned to work on the Page Galley, along the Rappahannock River. When the Revolutionary War started, that is where they were, on the Page Galley, working as Seamen. They were about twenty-two and nineteen years of age, at the time of the war. In 1777, they signed on as Seamen in the fight against the British. One benefit of signing as soldiers was that they were to be free from their indentures. They remained on the Galley for another year, before transferring to the Dragon Ship, a larger vessel.

The Dragon Ships first patrol was on the Rappahannock River, shortly after it was built by Fielding Lewis. Although the ship was commissioned by George Washington, the hands that actually built it were slaves. More blacks served on the Dragon than on any other Ship. The Dragon was a Medium sized ship, and engaged in combat only once, along the Rappahannock River. There were other Lewis family members on the Dragon Ship, one of whom, Benjamin Lewis, was the brother of John Lewis. The family of John Lewis owned property and plantations throughout Spotsylvania County.

Benjamin may have been an Uncle to Charles and Ambrose, yet closer to their age, than his brother John Lewis. Charles and Benjamin lived in Richmond Virginia in close proximity to each other, after the Revolutionary War. Another relative of the brothers, on the Dragon was Seamen, John Chew. He lost an arm when the Dragon was attacked by a British War Ship. In 1779, Ambrose and Charles completed their service as Seamen and signed on as Soldiers with the Second Virginia Regiment.

As Soldiers, the brothers fought at The Battle of Camden South Carolina. During the battle, Ambrose was shot nine times, and bayoneted clean through before being taken prisoner. He was then held on a British Prison Ship until the end of the war, which thanks to The Siege of Yorktown was not too long. Many of the soldiers deserted once they saw the strength of the British, but Ambrose waded in and fought valiantly. It is not clear whether Charles and Benjamin were imprisoned with Ambrose, but they were together after the war.

After the Revolutionary War Charles Lewis owned property in, and was one of the Free Mulattoes businessmen, at Rockett's Landing in Richmond Virginia. He also owned property in Richmond, as well as in Northumberland County. My belief is that his white Uncle, Benjamin Lewis was his front man, who assisted him in some of his business dealings. Charles may have been an excellent businessman, but he was not white, and lived in Colonial Virginia. It is doubtful that, given the times, Charles was doing business without a white man somewhere in the picture.

Although Ambrose eventually lived in Fredericksburg, after the War he was in King George County. He may have gone there to stay with his mother or another relative until he got on his feet. By 1790, Ambrose was one of only fifty-nine "Free Mulattos", living in Fredericksburg. He and his wife, Fanny Williams, raised children in Fredericksburg, before he moved to Alexandria Virginia in 1811. Before going to Alexandria, Ambrose worked as a Drayman, in Fredericksburg and had several cases against Ship Captains for payment.

Charles and Ambrose Lewis were not typical of the Free Persons of Color in Colonial Virginia. They have extensive documentation, including military records, marriage records, census, and applications by heirs for Bounty Land. Ambrose has significant documentation due to his application for a pension from his service in the Revolutionary War. Charles was more mobile than Ambrose was, and appears to have held business interests in Northumberland, Alexandria, Fredericksburg, and Henrico Counties.

Even with the injuries, Ambrose hustled and worked to support his family, as a draymen, and Barber in Fredericksburg. He died in 1833, when he was about seventy-five years old. In 1834, his heirs,

Fanny, Francis, and Fanny Bundy, petitioned for his Revolutionary War Land Bounty. Charles Lewis heirs, Hannah and Nancy Lewis, also petitioned for his Land Bounty in 1834. Both families received Certificates of Land Bounty for their service.

AMBROSE LEWIS PENSION APPLICATIONS

Following are some of the documents from Ambrose Lewis, pension files. The documents list the dates of service and his application for a pension. Ambrose moved from Fredericksburg to Alexandria to apply for his military pension. The documents left behind by Ambrose tell a story of what life was like for him during and after the Revolutionary War.

After Ambrose Pension was suspended, he petitioned the Senate to have it restored. This may be why he moved to Alexandria with little or no money. He appeared before the Senate in DC, at least three times, to plead his case. On at least one occasion, Charles submitted a petition for a pension with Ambrose. Eventually, Ambrose was successful in his bid for a pension, but Charles pension was denied. After his death, the heirs of Charles continued to petition for his pension and were not successful.

The following statement is given in Ambrose' own words:

"District Court of Columbia, County of Washington, 24 Jan 1821, before the Circuit Court of the District of Columbia, for the County of Washington (being a Court of record established as such by the several acts of Congress concerning the District of Columbia)."

'I have no estate or property whatsoever, real, personal or mixed; I am not even in a condition to accept my necessary clothing & Bedding; for I have no bedding; And not as much clothing as is necessary.

I have no income whatever; except the pension or pensions to which I may be entitled under the several acts of congress before mentioned, or some or one of the same and the casual contributions of the charitable, to which I have been compelled to resort since the payment of my pension has been suspended.

I have no occupation except occasionally that of a barber; and am not able to pursue any regular occupation for a livelihood, in consequence of my age and infirmity; and wound in my leg received at The Battle of Camden which wound, the greater part of my time breaks out into an open ulcer; and is always in a condition to render me a cripple in that leg.

I have no family but a son about ten year of age, who is unable to contribute to my or his own support; the rest of my children are grown up and live to themselves."

Signed Ambrose Lewis.

After the declaration Ambrose' pension was restored.

In the District of Columbia on the 7 Apr. 1818, Ambrose stood before the Circuit Court of the United States, claiming his age to be 60, and that he was a resident of Alexandria Virginia. He was applying for a pension under, "an act to provide for persons engaged in the land and naval service of the United States in the Revolutionary War."

Ambrose did not own any property but leased land from John Benson on Princess Anne Street in Fredericksburg.

The lease started on 15 September 1788, and was to be renewed once a year.

"He was to pay Six shillings current money for every foot contained in the front of the parcel of ground upon Princess Ann Street, and the said Ambrose and his assignees will set up one of more houses suitable for his habitation and abode. The agreement is signed by John Chew as Clerk of the Court of Hustings."

The Fredericksburg heirs initiated intestate proceedings after the deaths of Charles and Ambrose. Fanny Lewis accompanied by her daughter Fanny, (Bundy); Charles wife, Susanna (Hannah), daughters Fanny, and Nancy Lewis, attended the hearing. They were successful and received One hundred acres each for Charles and Ambrose.

Executive Department, August 15, 1834:

"The heirs of Ambrose Lewis are allowed Land and Bounty for his services as a Seaman in the (Virginia) State Navy. Signed, Littleton Tazewell, Governor (Virginia). The undersigned, [the only heirs of Ambrose Lewis who was a sailor and a soldier of the Revolution] appointed John C. Mosby of Richmond, Virginia their Attorney."

Signed, Fanny Lewis and Hannah Lewis. Witness, John Metcalf, 11 July 1834. Acknowledged before John H. Wallace, J.P. Fredericksburg, and Virginia. Corporation of Fredericksburg, James Chew, Clerk of Hustings Court, certified that John Wallace was a J. P. Received of the Register, Warrant #8082 for 100 acres, issued December 20, 1834. Signed, John G. Mosby, Attorney

Fredericksburg Court, July 10, 1834. Certified that Fanny Lewis and Hannah Lewis are the only heirs of Ambrose Lewis dec'd. That Fanny and Hannah Lewis, Fanny Bundy and Nancy Lewis are the only heirs of Charles Lewis, dec'd. Copy Testes, James J. Chew, Clerk.

John James Chew, Clerk of Spotsylvania County, certified that Ambrose and Charles Lewis, brothers, died intestate. Testes, December 6, 1834. Children of Ambrose; 660L102 1. Francis Lewis; 660L103 2. Hannah Lewis: Children of Charles; 660L104 Frances Lewis (a.k.a. Fanny Bundy); 2. Nancy Lewis"

*Note: Rodham Kenner, sailor in the Virginia Navy during the Revolutionary War, left heirs Phoebe Dillon, Cynthia Lewis, Sally Chew, Ely Chew, and Nancy Chew, who were also stated to be heirs of Ambrose Lewis.

In his pension application, Ambrose mentions a ten-year-old son, who is in his care. The son may have been William Berry Lewis, who by 1833 would have been a grown man. Fanny Lewis was still alive and living in Fredericksburg during that time. However, by his own admission Ambrose had little but the clothes on his back and some bedding in Alexandria. He also mentioned depending on the charity of others, possibly even his brother Charles.

DOCUMENTS OF CHARLES LEWIS:

1. On May 22 1792, Capt. Markham certifies that Charles Lewis entered with him in the Navy on 1 April 1777 and served three years. William Biggers witnessed Captain Markham (Captain of the Dragon Ship) Signature on the document.[39]

2. In the First Census of the United States, 1782 [page 112], Charles Lewis is listed as the owner of a property in Wardship No. 2. His tenants were Charles Hay, Free Mulatto, and Kate Robertson, 26: Nancy Lewis (Charles daughter), a slave, tithable or hire; and one horse.

3. Charles and his wife Susannah were selling land in The City of Richmond to John Hague on June 13, 1796 [lot 212]. It is in the East End of the city near the James River. The land is located on Water Street in an area known as the Rockets.

4. 1807–1809, Monday, December 5, 1808 "Mr. Dawson presented a petition of Ambrose Lewis and Charles Lewis, of the State of Virginia, praying compensation for their respective services as soldiers in the Continental Army, during the Revolutionary War with Great Britain, which the petitioners have not yet received, owing to the circumstances therein enumerated."

   "The under mentioned petition and memorial heretofore presented, were again, presented, and referred to the Committee on Revolutionary Claims, Viz:

   "By Mr. Garland of Virginia: The petition of the heirs of Colonel Charles Lewis, presented December 11, 1833. Mr. Dawson presented a petition of Ambrose Lewis, praying for arrearages of the pension heretofore granted him."

   "Ordered that the said petition be referred to the Committee of Claims."

Nancy Lewis and Family
   In 1815 Nancy Lewis appeared before The Fredericksburg Court, where a Mrs. Hildruss attested to the fact that James Lewis, and Milley Lewis, were known to be Nancy's' children, and that

they were born free, as was Nancy Lewis. The document is made on March 4, 1815.

Nancy Lewis' registration included her son James and her daughter Milley. Mrs. Hildruss was Nancy's employer, and gave testimony that Nancy was born free. Nancy's testimony without her white employer would not have been sufficient. Mrs. Hildruss states that Nancy worked for her, and that she was born free. She also states that she knew, James and Milley to be the children of Nancy.

On at least one occasion, Nancy filed charges of battery against Mrs. Hildruss, who whipped her. She was a housekeeper for Mrs. Hildruss, and was accused of stealing from her. Mrs. Hildruss punishment for battery against Nancy Lewis was a two-dollar fine, which was dismissed. On one occasion, Nancy was sentenced to receive ten lashings on her back, for stealing from Mrs. Hildruss. Yet she was required to return to this employer, and maintain a job.

The daughter of Nancy Lewis, Maria Lewis-Jackson, was my direct ancestor, and the daughter-in-law of Patty Bowden-Jackson. She was married to Patty's son, Samuel Jackson, and is listed Free Negro Registry for 1822. Nancy stood bond for Maria (her daughter) when she and Samuel Jackson were married in 1813. The couple lived in the house owned by James and Patty Bowden-Jackson, on Princess Anne Street. Prior to slavery, Lower Princess Anne Street was where most of the Free Blacks lived in Fredericksburg. Another street that many free blacks lived on was Liberty Street, which is not too far from Princess Anne Street.

As a Mulatto, Maria was required to serve an Indenture until she was thirty-one years of age. Samuel Jackson died about 1830, and Maria died sometime prior to 1839, leaving young children. Nancy Lewis took over raising her grandchildren, after the death of her daughter. There were three children, Elizabeth, Anne, and Walter Samuel, who was an infant. When Maria, and Samuels' daughter, Elizabeth Jackson married (Robert Pinn), in April of 1838, her uncle William Lewis, was listed as her guardian. William Lewis may have been the same person attesting to his grandfather, Charles Lewis freeing a slave in Northumberland County.

Maria Lewis – Free Negro Registry 1822
Virginia, Sct. No. 177

In pursuance of an act of assembly entitled: "An Act for regulating the Police of Towns in this Commonwealth, and to restrain the practice of Negroes going at large,"

I Robert Smith Chew, Clerk of the Court of Hustings for the town and corporation of Fredericksburg, do hereby certify, that Maria Jackson, formerly Maria Lewis, a Mulatto woman, aged 28 years, Five feet Seven inches high, who was Born Free,___, is registered in my office, agreeable to the directions of the above recited act____ Certified this 12th day of June 1822, under my hand and under the seal of the Said Corporation's Chew, CCHF; Attested A. Walker__ One of the Magistrates in the Town of Fredericksburg.

The Free Negro Registry required that any Person of Color (Negro, Mulatto, Free Black, etc.), appear before a Magistrate with proof of their status, usually a letter from a white property owner. Once proof was established the name, age, color, height, and weight were recorded. The records were numbered and recorded, allowing anyone who required access to the document. The records were public, and the intention was to have a record Free Persons and their movements.

In the following "Free Negro Registry" for Alexandria Virginia, Charles Lewis is listed as the former owner of a Francis or Frank, and Fanny Williams. After her emancipation, Fanny mentioned became the wife of Ambrose Lewis.

Registration No. 153:

3 Oct 1825, Negro Fanny: "Fanny is about 60 years old, has a dark complexion, and is 5 feet ¾ inches tall, she was manumitted by Charles Lewis, as appears by deed of manumission recorded in Liber C No. 2, folio 116

Registration No. 154:

3 Oct 1825, Francis William: "Frances" or Frank is about 22 years old, has a dark complexion, and is 5 feet 8 ½ inches

tall. Charles Lewis freed him, as appears by the deed of manumission recorded in Liber C No. 2, folio 116

Registration No. 210:

3 Aug 1847, Francis Williams is about 44 years old, 5 feet 8 ½ inches tall, of a brownish-black color, with no visible marks. Williams was emancipated by Charles Lewis as appears by a previous registration.[40]

The children of Charles Lewis are listed in the, Pioneer Lewis Family, as Francis, John, William, and Nancy. Zachary Lewis married Betty Smith, and it appears that the Chews were related to the Smiths. Robert Smith Chew may have been a relative of Charles and Ambrose. John Chew (a Smith relative), is listed as a relative of Ambrose Lewis. One of the Registries lists a Robert Lewis attesting to the information in their document. The document was the "Free Negro Registry" for William Lewis [Registry No. 170], who gave Bond so that Maria Lewis, daughter of Nancy Lewis could marry Samuel Jackson. The other scenario is that William was the father of Maria Lewis. Marrying cousins seemed to be a common practice in the white and Mulatto Lewis families.

JACKSON AND LEWIS FAMILY IN FREDERICKSBURG

Maria (Lewis) and husband Samuel Jackson owned property in Fredericksburg. The property was left by Samuel's mother, Patty Bowden-Jackson when she died in 1830. Maria worked as a seamstress, while her husband Samuel Jackson, was a laborer for Charles Yates. In 1830 Samuel Jackson Willed his real & personal property to his children Elizabeth and Ann Maria (Jackson) Bundy got the got home and land; Walter B. Jackson, his son, got land.

According to white Lewis family members, Charles and Ambrose Lewis were open secrets of the Lewis family. This may be why their names were included in, the book, Pioneer Lewis Families. Ambrose and Charles were names that were common in the Smith family (descended from an Ambrose Smith) that intermarried with the Zachary Lewis family of Spotsylvania County.

In his will dated, 19 Oct 1780, John Lewis names as his executors "my brothers," Zachary, Wallace and Benjamin Lewis and "my brothers-in-law" Nicholas, Charles and William Lewis; and my friends, Fielding Lewis and Joseph Jones (Fielding Lewis commissioned the Dragon Ship). Benjamin Lewis lived in close proximity to Charles and served as a Seaman on board the Dragon Ship.

Larkin Chew had a long association with the Lewis family. The Chews served as Magistrates and Clerks of the Court for many years. Larkin Chew signed documents attesting that Ambrose was born free, and a resident, and that he served in the Revolutionary War. His brother John Chew lost an arm serving on board the Dragon Ship, during the Revolutionary War. Larkin's father John Chew also signed sworn statements and gave testimony to the character of Ambrose and his family.

The relationship stretched from a period after the Revolutionary War, until after Ambrose death when John Chew signed documents for Ambrose and his family who remained in Fredericksburg. He gave a sworn statement for Ambrose when he needed a reference for his service in the war. Charles daughter Nancy is registered in the Fredericksburg Free Negro Registry. Fanny Lewis is also registered in the Fredericksburg Registry.

Margaret Givens-Green may be a descendant of Ambrose Lewis, through his son, William Berry Lewis. She is related to a William Berry, who may have been a son of Ambrose Lewis. He dropped his last name, and became a fugitive, traveling through the Underground Railroad with his wife and children.

Statement from Margaret Givens- Green, descendants of Ambrose Lewis:

"Berry (William) was my great-great grandfather, who was born a free man in Virginia (I have the census'). I was told (stories passed down) that Berry's son, John (my great-grandfather-documented), was named, after Berry's father. I also heard that Berry named his first child and daughter, Josephine (born in Virginia) after Berry's mulatto grandmother. Again, through stories passed down, I heard that Berry's son, James' middle name was the same as Berry's father.

In the last six months, I gained proof (by way of a marriage license from Colchester, (Ontario) that James' middle name was "Ambrose." I know you know the pain-staking search process but I am becoming more and more convinced (with a great uncle's declaration years ago that his grandfather's (Berry) father was in the Revolutionary War and was on a "Ship Dragon" and that he was shot and stabbed with a big sword."[41]

In Fredericksburg (1844), there was a William Lewis, who was accused of writing a letter, and stealing from a white man. He was sentenced to jail, and would have been under scrutiny as a Negro who was literate. Margaret Givens-Green and her family eventually came back to the United States and settled in Michigan.

The Lewis and Jackson family resided on the same street in Fredericksburg, Princess Anne. The street housed the Minor, Jackson, Lucas, and Lewis families, the families lived on Princess Anne Street facing the Rappahannock River. It is interesting to note that these families had a clear view of the slave ships coming into the slave port in Fredericksburg. The slaves in the City of Fredericksburg proper were primarily used as house servants. They also had more freedom of movement then slaves living on a plantation.

Some were also required to serve apprenticeships from the age of twelve to twenty-one, and were paid fees. The apprenticeship could be set by the courts, especially when the person was poor. The son of Samuel and Maria Lewis-Jackson, Walter Samuel Jackson, was ordered by the courts to serve an apprenticeship in 1844. He served an apprenticeship as a carpenter until he was twenty-one years of age. Later, Samuel Walter-Jackson moved to Washington DC, and was a prominent carpenter there. He married Anne Riva in Fredericksburg before moving to Washington DC. He was the brother of my direct ancestor, Elizabeth Jackson-Pinn.

QUASI FREE PERSONS OF COLOR IN FREDERICKSBURG VIRGINIA

Living in Colonial Virginia as a Free Person of Color, had many pitfalls, which included being assaulted or imprisoned. Following are several cases where Free Persons of Color were charged with offenses, or assaulted. My ancestors were assaulted and abused on several occasions by their employers. On June 14, 1821, my ancestor Nancy Lewis, and another Free Black, Maria Washington, were taken to court, and accused of an affray (fighting). They were jailed and after being found guilty received ten lashes.

An entry date for the Mayor's Court Order Book Records:
"May 6, 1822, Peace warrant issued against John Cruson for an assault upon the person of Nancy Lewis, a free woman of color, for beating & whipping her with a cow skin whip in an unlawful & cruel manner."
"May 9, 1822 William Bell, mariner, was arrested by order of the Magistrates in open court for an assault upon the person of Nancy Lewis & committed for the want of security until discharged by due course of law."
"In 1823 Nelly Star was arrested under my warrant for abusing Maria Jackson and beating her girl. On hearing the testimony in behalf of the Commonwealth, she was sentenced to receive ten lashes, which was communted by the payment of a fine of two dollars, for the benefit of the informers."
"In 1817 Nancy Lewis, and James Lewis (her son), were accused of receiving stolen goods. The stolen goods they were accused of stealing was a slave, named Jacob, who was the property of Samuel Owens."

In 1827, my direct ancestor, James Jackson, the husband of Patty Bowden-Jackson was taken before the Courts in Fredericksburg.

"James Jackson, a free man of color, having been charged before me with abusive and indecorous language towards Mrs. Frances Taylor, was sentenced to receive ten lashes, upon his bare back & to pay costs."

In 1825 the Fredericksburg Court Posted an Insolvency List (most are Mulatto):
Insolvency List for 1824

Gibbs, James
Howard, William
Lewis, Nancy (daughter of Charles Lewis)
Minor, Betsey
Moss, Jack
Peirce, Lydia
Soleather, Nancy
Soleather, Betsey
Williams, Maria
Webb, Letty
Washington, Maria

FREDERICKSBURG VIRGINIA LIST OF FREE NEGROES 1801

Joseph Francis (Mulatto) (24) – laborer
- Sarah Grace (Mulatto) – stemmer
- William Grace (Negro) (18) – shoemaker
- Betsey Carter (Mulatto) (16) – washerwoman
- Fanny Richardson (dark Mulatto) (53) – washerwoman
- Lucy Richardson (Negro) (24) – washerwoman
- Phyllis (light Negro) (36) - tobacco stemmer
- Maria McGuy (Mulatto) (18) - tobacco stemmer
- John Pinn (Mulatto) (26) – drayman
- William Bundy (Negro) (24) – drayman
- Barnett Moore (Negro) (22) – carpenter
- Christian Cook (Negro) (33) – washerwoman
- Samuel Henry (Negro) (35) – gardener
- William Jones (Mulatto) (38) – drayman
- Charlotte (Mulatto) (55) – washerwoman
- Daniel Cooper (Negro) (27) – laborer
- Anna Maria Richardson (dark Mulatto) (19) – washerwoman
- Patsey Richardson (dark Mulatto) (27) – washerwoman
- Hanna Plum Richardson (dark Mulatto) (14) – washerwoman
- Catharine Bundy (dark Mulatto) (20) – washerwoman
- Elizabeth Bundy (light Negro) (34) – washerwoman

- Lucy Wilmore (Mulatto) (27) – washerwoman
- Armistead Stocus (light Negro) (33) – drayman
- James West (Negro) (30) – blacksmith
- Elijah Deane (dark Mulatto) (22) – laborer
- Alice (Mulatto) (48) – washerwoman
- Jane Rollins (dark Mulatto) (43) – washerwoman
- Sally Rollins (dark Mulatto) (15) – washerwoman
- Winney (dark Mulatto) (26) – washerwoman
- Patsey Bowden (dark Mulatto) (55) – spinner
- Elizabeth Howard (dark Mulatto) (22) – washerwoman
- Aminadab Booker (dark Mulatto) (45) – laborer
- Robert Weedon (Negro) (54) – drayman
- Rawleigh Thomas (Mulatto) (30) – laborer
- Sally Rollings (light Negro) (40) – washerwoman
- Lucy Rollings (light Negro) (17) – washerwoman
- William Bedman (Mulatto) (23) – laborer
- William Lewis (Mulatto) (24) – drayman
- Barbara Hollinger (light Mulatto) (25) – washerwoman
- Eppa Laws (light Mulatto) (31) – shoemaker
- James Furguson (Negro) (29) – barber
- Sarah Lewis (bright Mulatto) (66) – washerwoman
- Milley Lewis (Mulatto) (26) – spinner
- Ned Webb (Negro) (24) - baker or seafarer
- Frankey Webb (dark Mulatto) (40) - washerwoman & stemmer
- Hannah Webb (dark Mulatto) (26) - washerwoman & cook
- Polly Lewis (Mulatto) (16) - washerwoman & stemmer
- Elcy Cook (Mulatto) (38) - washerwoman, seamstress & spinner
- Betsey Webb (bright Mulatto) (18) - lives with Mr. McArthur
- Rachael Sturr (KG) (bright Mulatto) (18) - seamstress & washerwoman
- Kizzy Sturr (KG) (dark Mulatto) (24) - seamstress & washerwoman
- Martha Bowden (Mulatto) (52) - seamstress & washerwoman

- Jane Deane (KG) (light Mulatto) (24) - seamstress & washerwoman
- Frances Deane (KG) (dark Mulatto) (50) - seamstress & washerwoman
- Nelly Sturr (KG) (dark Mulatto) (17) - seamstress & stemmer
- Alice Sturr (KG) (dark Mulatto) (20) - seamstress & stemmer
- Thomas Sturr (dark Mulatto) (15) - cabinetmaker with Glasgow
- Ann Richardson (Mulatto) (20) – washerwoman
- Gawing Evans (KG) (Negro) (21) – blacksmith
- Jenney Mann (Mulatto) (42) – stemmer
- Barbary Payne (Mulatto) [no age given] - Steamer Locality Fredericksburg

⌘ ⌘ ⌘

CHAPTER ELEVEN

≠ ≠

VIRGINIA PINN AND EVANS IN AMHERST COUNTY

The Natives on the Eastern Shore of Virginia were the Wicomico, a tribe tributary to the Powhatan. They were Natives who depended on Fishing and Hunting for their existence, and inhabited the area for at least ten thousand years. The division of the Wicomico land put split the tribe between borders of Maryland and Virginia. Then it was divided again, into the Wicomico Parish District (Episcopalian), and the Christ Church Parish (Anglican). Although the Pinn's resided at Indiantown in Lancaster County, they remained members of the Wicomico Parish Church.

In the book, Indian Island, the following statement is made:

"The Pinn's were linked to the Redcrosses and Evans as Indian Derivatives. Rawley Penn (Pinn), was the father of six "Mulattoes," the official name of Indian Derivatives and other non-whites at the time of the National Census in 1785. One of his children, Anna Penn, married Thomas Evans, and James Penn (Pinn), married Nancy Redcross…"

The names Redcross, Penn (Pinn), Evans, Branham, and Johns were known to have been resident in the country before the Cherokee and Choctaw-Chickasaw delegates made their annual journey to see "the Great White Father."[42]

The Pinn Indians were a mixture of Chicawane and Wicomico Indians who were tributary to the Powhatan. They were some of the first Natives, to be enslaved by Europeans in the area. John Pinn, the first identifiable Pinn, appears to be mixed raced, Native/White. That would be John Pinn, who owned land in Lancaster County. Some of his descendants are identified as Indian, while others were Mulatto. Natives in the area were either members of Wicomico Parish Church in Northumberland County, or Christ Church Parish in Lancaster County.

This was the reality of Colonization for the Natives, some of whom intermixed with whites and others with Africans, or Free Blacks in the area. The intermarriage (and mixing) of Natives and blacks was a matter of concern for those in power. In 1784 Thomas Jefferson stated that, "The population of living Indians in Virginia includes just three or four, male Mattaponi "and they have more negro than Indian blood in them, ten to twelve, Pamunkey, and not a male left among the Nottoway." Although Natives were intermixing with Europeans, it was less of an economic threat, than an increase in Free Blacks. The laws of Colonial Virginia set the status of the child according to the mother. Eventually Jefferson's fears would spark laws intended to halt the intermixing of Natives and blacks.

The Pinn surname is well documented from 1650 on in Northumberland and Lancaster County. In 1649, John Pine (Pinn) is documented as owning and farming several hundred acres of land in Lancaster County Virginia. John Pine purchased land in Lancaster County in partnership with William Keegan, from Edward Lilly on 7 Sep 1652. Around 21 Mar 1652/3 Pine received a cow in partnership with William Newson. By 1667, John had a plantation called "The Island" on the Corotoman River. He would sell a small amount of this acreage as a right of way for a ferry across the river, as the county grew. In addition, during the seventeenth century, another Pine, a male named Francy Pine farmed in Lancaster County.[43]

There is a Land Grant to Wm. Newsom, Thomas Sacks, Myles Batesby and John Pinn, of eight-hundred acres called Island neck on N side Rappahannock near Corotomen, for transporting 16 persons.

- 29 Jan 1649/50. Myles Battersby sells his interest in his land to Newsom and Pinn,
- 21 March 1652/3. Newsom and Pinn (here as Pine) assign their interests in this land to Thomas Sacks.
- 22 March 1652/3. land Grant to Wm. Newsom, Thomas Sacks, Myles Battersby and John Pinn, 550 acres on N side Rappahannock River in Northumberland County; Battersby assigns his interest in this 550 acres to Wm. Newsom and Jno. Pine, 22 March 1642. (This date in the original is an error and should be 1652/3).[44]

By the 1740's, Pine had become Pinn, and the Pinn Surname was clearly identified as Native American. On May 13, 1748, the Lancaster County Court Justices apprenticed Hezziah Pinn to Thomas Hubbard and his wife, Margaret. Hezziah was the orphaned daughter of the late "Indian" Harry.

"Mr. and Mrs. Hubbard were to teach Hezziah the female needlecrafts of sewing, knitting and spinning. They were also to teach her to read."[45]

- On August 25, 1754, the Northumberland County Courthouse approved the following documents:
- To Ezekiel Hayden of Lancaster County for taking up John Pinn, a servant man belonging to Richard Hudnall of this county, 90 lbs. Tobacco.
- To William Garner of this county for taking up Raleigh (Rawley) Pinn, a servant boy belonging to Richard Seldon of Lancaster County, 90 lbs. Tobacco. [46]

John Pinn I, may have been a brother to Rawley and Robert. By the time, the indenture began Robert Pinn I, (Rawley and Johns' father, was probably deceased. By 1758, Margaret Pinn was in Lancaster County, and signed Robert Pinn II to serve an apprenticeship as a Cooper.

Robert Pinn I, born about 1710, was presented by the Churchwardens of Wicomico Parish, Northumberland County on 16 Aug 1733 for absenting himself from church. He was in Lancaster County on 13 Jan 1744 when his son, Robert, was bound to Thomas Dogget as an apprentice Cooper. He was documented in 1733 by the Churchwardens of Wicomico Parish [Northumberland County] for absenting himself from church. Robert may have had a brother named David Pinn who was born about 1720 and was taxed in Benjamin George's Christ Church This same Parish identified David Pinn, as an Indian (Indian David).

- Robert Pinn I, and his wife Margaret were the parents of Robert Pinn II , Born about 1740; Rawley Pinn, born about 1742, and John Pinn I, born about 1745.
- Robert Pinn II was taxable on three tithes and four cattle in Lancaster County in 1787. His son John Pinn II left a pension record application giving information about his family.
- In his pension application, John Pinn II, states that; his father Robert and brothers, James and Billy, served in the Revolutionary War and participated in The Siege at Yorktown. He described his father as a "Mustee (Mestezo)", and his mother, Ann as Cherokee. He, John Pinn II, married Ann Cassaday, 12 Sep 1785, in Lancaster County Virginia.[47]

EXCERPT OF JOHN PINN PENSION FILE:

"On this 28th day of October in the year 1842, Personally appeared in open court before the Commonwealth of Massachusetts, Suffolk County, 29 October 1842., John Pin a resident of Chelsea in the County and state Aforesaid; aged eighty-years…, That the said John Pin together with his late Father, Robert Pin and brothers, Billy and James or Jim Pin, were soldiers in the army of the Revolutionary War and that his father, Robert Pin, Aforesaid and himself served together in Captain William Yarby's Company of Virginia Artillery and the Regiment commanded by Col. Williams.

That himself was a powder Boy, and attached to Gun No. 5, under the command of said Captain Yarby during which service he was at the Siege of Yorktown in Virginia when Lord Cornwallis surrendered his army to General Washington that during the cannonade on that occasion he, the said John received several wounds one from an enemies spent cannon ball, which injured his right ankle and the other from a musket shot through the left leg.

The declarant further states that he is a descendant of the Aborigines of America that his father was a Mustee and his mother a Cherokee. They were inhabitants of Lancaster County Virginia at a place called "Indian Town" near Carter's Creek in said County. That he is a seaman by occupation in which employment he has been engaged ever since the termination of the Revolutionary War which calling he still follows.

The declarant further states that soon after the termination of the Revolutionary War, his father, Robert Pinn (II), (Rawley Pinn's brother), obtained from the United States the quantity of Bounty Land due on account of the services of himself and his three sons in the army amongst whom was the declarant and his brothers, Jim (James) & Billy Pin, who as he believes served in the Rifle Corps under Colonial Morgan. The former of who was killed when in spy service.

John Pinn II married Anne Cassidy, 12 September 1785 in Northumberland County, Virginia bond. He was living in Boston, Massachusetts on 28 October 1842 when he applied for a pension for his services in the Revolution. He had moved to Boston about 1792 and married Nancy Coffin about ten years later. He testified that his brothers Jim and William also served and that Jim died in the service. He was described as "a colored man - apparently of Indian Origin," and is a person of good report amongst our mercantile community both here and at Salem (Massachusetts)."[48]

The application was filed in Massachusetts in 1842, where he lived after the Revolutionary War. The document is a personal testimony of John Pinn (II) and his life prior to and after the War. The importance of the document is the statement of John Pinn regarding his ethnicity and that he, his father, and brothers service at Yorktown. John Pinn fought along with his father, Robert Pinn II, and his brothers', Billy and James. Also at Yorktown was John

Pinn's Uncle, Rawley Pinn, whose unit marched to Yorktown from Amherst County. There is an "Indian" notation on the pension file of John Pinn II, identifying him as a Native of America. On the file, John states that his mother was Cherokee, and his father a Mustee."

RAWLEY PINN SETTLER ON BUFFALO RIDGE

Some time before 1773, Rawley Pinn left Lancaster County and traveled through Lunenburg, Rockbridge, and Nelson Counties. Rawley and Sarah Evans married around 1774, probably in Lunenburg County, where she owned property. They signed deeds of purchase and sale, of land in Amherst County, the last around 1801. Both signed their names, and probably learned to read and write at a Mission School. The Mission Schools in Colonial Virginia were funded by and connected to the Church.

One of the Indian Mission Schools was located at the College of William and Mary, in Williamsburg Virginia. Rawley was a Minute Man, in Amherst County, prior to the Revolutionary War. When the war started, Rawley became part of a unit, which marched to Yorktown. The Unit combined with Marquis De Lafayette, and his soldiers. They fought together at the, Siege of Yorktown, a battle that saw the defeat of General Cornwallis.

The land owned by Sarah Evans, was left to her by her father, Charles Evans, prior to his death. The land was often divided, by surveyors, and set in adjoining states, and/or counties. This is what happened in Lexington Parish, when Rawley owned property by Porridge Creek. The land was cut off, with half going to Nelson County, and the other half remaining in Amherst County. With the Evans family, Brunswick County became Lunenburg County, and parts of Lunenburg County were changed into Amherst County. Sarah Evans lines appear to be Native/White, which led to the description of Mulatto, and Colored. The property Sarah owned was left to her by her father, Charles Evans, who lived in Brunswick County.

Prior to marrying Rawley Pinn, Sarah was known by two last names, Redcross and Evans. The Redcross name may have come from the relationship with the mother of her half-brother, Daniel

Redcross. On 12 Sep 1777, Daniel Redcross, left half of his estate to John Epps, and the other half to his brother Charles Evans. There is also a familial relationship between the Brunswick County, Epps, Evans, and Redcross.

EVANS OF BRUNSWICK COUNTY VIRGINIA

Charles Evans, born say 1696, was sued for debt in Brunswick County court by Littlebury Eppes in December 1735 [Orders 1732-37, 68]. He was called "Charles Evans a mulatto" in December 1746 in Lunenburg County when the court dismissed charges brought against him by Andrew Bresslar [Orders 1746-48, 81]. He received a patent on 20 August 1747 for 120 acres on Stith's Creek in the part of Brunswick County which became Lunenburg County in 1748 and Mecklenburg County in 1765 [Patents 28:135].

He was taxable in Lunenburg County in the list of Lewis Deloney in 1748, taxable in the list of Field Jefferson in 1751 with his son Tom [Bell, *Sunlight on the Southside*, 68, 166] and taxable with Thomas and Major Evans in 1752 [Tax List 1748-52, 1]. He petitioned the Lunenburg County court in May 1753 to be exempt from personal taxes, but was rejected "for reasons appearing to the Court" [Orders 1753-54, 113]. He was granted 38 acres in Lunenburg County in the fork of Miles Creek and Dockery's Creek on 23 July 1753 [Patents 31:337].

He left a 22 March 1760 Brunswick County, Virginia will (signing), proved 27 October 1760, leaving his "Manor" Plantation on the south side of Dockery's Creek to his son Major Evans, left an equal quantity to his son Charles Evans and left the residue of his land on the south side of Dockery's Creek to son Dick Evans on condition they give twenty pounds or 100 acres of land to his youngest son Erasmus. He left a bed and furniture to his daughters Sarah and Joice, but left only a shilling to his "undutiful" son Thomas [WB 3:375-6].

He died before June 1760 when a suit against him in Lunenburg County court abated by his death [Orders 1759-61, 136]. On 18 October 1764 Sarah and Richard Evans sold about 39 acres in the fork of Miles and Dockery's Creek in Mecklenburg County which was land they had been given by Charles Evans [DB 1:514]. And on the same date Sarah, Charles and Major Evans sold 120 acres on Stith's Creek in Lunenburg County adjoining Philip Morgan [DB 8:356].[49]

His children were:

i. Thomas[3], born say 1734.
ii. Major[1], born say 1735.
iii. Charles[2], born say 1737.
iv. Richard[1], born say 1740.
v. Sarah Evans-Pinn
vi. Joyce

THE SAPONI ON BUFFALO RIDGE

The Saponi who are Siouan, were a tribe that lived in the Southeastern United States for thousands of years. They, like the Monacan are a Siouan (Sioux), Group. The Evans and Epps are from Brunswick County, and believed to be Saponi. The Saponi were located in Northern North Carolina, and in Brunswick County in Virginia. The Native lands were divided, and then divided again into counties. This caused dispersion, of the tribe from their homeland.

"Some of the Saponi moved to the region controlled by the Catawba in present day South Carolina, but by 1733 they had moved back into Virginia. Some eventually moved into Pennsylvania and finally to Canada, where they were adopted by a division of the Iroquois Confederacy. Others moved to North Carolina. Some settled in what later became Louisa County, Virginia, and others occupied the region around Bear Mountain in present day Amherst County.

There in 1790 William Johns, (designated a Free Person of Color), married Molly Evans and Ned Branham married Molly's Sister Nancy. William Johns was sometimes referred to as, "Portugue." These individuals, along with Raleigh Penn (Rawley Pinn), represented the primary family groups that would dominate this community for generations."[50]

By 1783, he is listed as white, in the Personal Property Tax List, of Amherst County, living with eight others. In 1785, he is listed as a Mulatto, living in Amherst County, with eight others. Many of the band that settled on the Ridge were displaced Natives who wanted to live their lives as their ancestors had. The Pinn family left records telling of their accomplishments and providing a look into life in the 1700's. The band that settled Amherst County had a cohesive community centered on family, religion, education, and work.

The Natives who settled on Buffalo Ridge in Amherst County assimilated into the dominant culture and were reclassified as "Mulatto." Some of the "Mulattos" living on Buffalo Ridge lived prosperous lifestyles, owning land and even having a house servant or two at one point. If it were not for the pressures of the outside community, this life could have been passed on to future generations. Instead, within several generations, the land was lost and those who could not leave suffered economic hardships.[51]

REDCROSS, EPPS, EVANS, & PINN CONNECTIONS

The surname of my ancestor, Sarah Evans (wife of Rawley Pinn), was at first, difficult to prove. Many years ago, someone said her last name was most likely Evans. I know that there was intermarrying going on but, Ann Pinn, Sarah's daughter married, Thomas Evans. However, after researching the Evans' family I saw that there was a familial relationship. Sarah Evans, had a brother named Thomas, who was born in 1734. The Thomas Evans that married Ann Pinn was a distant relative. The, Rule of Thumb (at least in our family), was no relationships with cousins less then three generations removed. If they had the same last name, it was out of the question, even after three generations.

My ancestor, James Pinn's first wife was, Nancy Redcross, but it does not appear she was a close relative. Some of the Evans and Redcross families were related, but the Redcross surname denotes a tribe more than a family. The name Redcross was given to denote that they were Christian Natives.

If there is a relationship, hopefully, it is beyond that third generation cousin line. It appears as if the, Evans, Pinn, and Redcross families, were within the, "Three-Generation Rule." The upside is that they were Native Americans intermarrying with other Natives.

1. "Hannah Evans, born say 1753, was living in Lexington Parish, Amherst County, on 6 July 1789 when the court ordered the overseers of the poor to bind her illegitimate "Molatter" son Thomas Evans to Samuel Brown to learn the trade of blacksmith [Orders 1787-90, 499].
   She was the mother of:
   i. ?Nancy, born say 1769, married Edward Branham (Brandon), 6 December 1790 Amherst County Marriage Bond.
   ii. Thomas, born say 1772, named in the Amherst County will of his grandfather Thomas Evans. He, a blacksmith, married Ann Penn (Pinn), daughter of Rawley and Sarah Pinn, 2 November 1795 Amherst County bond. Thomas was taxable in Amherst County from 1800 to 1810, called a "man of color" in 1811 and head of an Amherst County household of 7 "other free" in 1810; He was listed on South River in Rockbridge County in 1813 as a "Black" male with two "Black" females over the age of sixteen [Waldrep, 1813 Tax List]."

2. ?Daniel Redcross, born say 1752, bound to John Evans/ Epps by the churchwardens of Cumberland Parish, Lunenburg County, on 10 December 1767 [Orders 1766-69, fol.122]. He was taxable in the Lunenburg County household of John Evans in 1772 and 1773 and called Daniel Evans in John's household in 1775 [Bell, *Sunlight on the Southside,* 304, 324, 354]. He left a 12 September 1777 Lunenburg County will, proved 10 June 1779, leaving half his estate to his brother Charles Evans and the remainder to John Epps [WB 3:26].

3. Erasmus, born say 1745.

4. Thomas Evans, born say 1710, was called "Thomas Evans (otherwise lately called &c)" in Amherst County court on 2 September 1766 when the sheriff attached a fork of his for a debt he owed Samuel Woods. He was added to Henry Bell's road gang on, 7 December 1767. In December the court ordered his male laboring tithables to keep the road in repair from Buffalo River to Stovall's Road and ordered that Thomas be surveyor thereof [Orders 1766-9, 74, 233; 1773-82].

By his 28 June 1774 Amherst County will, proved 5 September 1774, he left to his son Benjamin his land and a horse as well as cattle and hogs for the use of his daughters Mary and Hannah and grandson Thomas as long as they abided together and left a shilling each to sons Charles, Thomas, William and Stanup (Stanhope) and daughter Nelly [WB 1:264-5].

He was the father of:

i. Charles, born say 1751, called son & heir-at-law of Thomas Evans, deceased, when he was summoned by the Amherst County court on 5 September 1774 to contest the will of his father [Orders 1773-82, 107].

ii. Thomas

iii. William

iv. Stanhope, born say 1740, granted 350 acres in Amherst County on both sides of Johns Branch, a north branch of Buffaloe River, on 14 July 1780 [Grants A, 1779-80, 634].

v. Nelly.

vi. Benjamin[1], born say 1749.

vii. Mary, born say 1751, perhaps the Mary Evans whose illegitimate daughter Sarah Evans was ordered bound by the churchwardens of Lexington Parish on 7 March 1785 [Orders 1784-7, 72], and perhaps identical to Molly Evans who was head of an Amherst County household of 2 "other free" in 1810 [VA:286].

viii. Hannah, born say 1753.

5   John Epps/Evans, born say 1735, was apparently the illegitimate son of a member of the Epps and Evans families. He was called John Evans in 1751 and 1752 when he was taxable in the Lunenburg County household of (his half-brother?) Thomas Evans [Bell, *Sunlight on the Southside*, 166, 193]. He was called John Epps in September 1752 when he and Margaret Evans were called as witnesses in the trial of Peter, a slave of Edward Epps, but he was called John Evans in January 1753 when he was paid for his attendance at the trial [Orders 1752-3, 249, 456].

He was called John Evans on 6 October 1761 when he purchased 400 acres on Flat Rock Creek jointly with Thomas Biddie for 60 pounds and on 3 August 1762; when he and Biddie allowed Ann Mitchell the use of the plantation to raise stock and grow corn or other grains during her natural life as long as she and her sons Richard and Isaac remained single. He was called John Epps when he and his wife Martha sold 299 acres of this land for 115 pounds on 8 January 1771 [DB 6:473; 7:321; 11:433].

He was called John Evans on 10 December 1767, when the Lunenburg County court ordered the Churchwardens of Cumberland Parish to bind Daniel Redcross to him and called "John Evans (alias Eppes)" on 13 April 1769 when the court ordered the churchwardens to bind Isham Harris (son of Martha Stewart) to him [Orders 1766-69, fol. 122, 202]. Isham Harris and Daniel Redcross were taxable in his Lunenburg County household in 1772 and 1773. Daniel was called Daniel Evans when he was taxable in his household in 1775.

Their children were:

i. Hannah Evans, born say 1753, was living in Lexington Parish, Amherst County, on 6 July 1789 when the court ordered the overseers of the poor to bind her illegitimate "Mulatto" son Thomas Evans to Samuel Brown to learn the trade of blacksmith [Orders 1787-90, 499].
    She was the mother of:

ii. Thomas , born say 1772, named in the Amherst County will of his grandfather Thomas Evans. He, a blacksmith, married Ann Penn, daughter of Rawley (Raleigh) and Sarah Pinn, 2 November 1795 Amherst County Bond. Thomas was taxable in Amherst County from 1800 to 1810, called a "man of color" in 1811 [PPTL 1782-1803, frames 481, 553, 587; 1804-23, frames 23, 167, 189, 210] and head of an Amherst County household of seven "other free" in 1810 [VA: 268]. He was listed on South River in Rockbridge County in 1813 as a "Black" male with two "Black" females over the age of sixteen [Waldrep, *1813 Tax List*].

6. Charles Evans, born say 1696, was sued for debt in Brunswick County court by Littlebury Epes in December 1735 [Orders 1732-37, 68]. He was called "Charles Evans a mulatto" in December 1746 in Lunenburg County when the court dismissed charges brought against him by Andrew Bresslar [Orders 1746-48, 81]. He received a patent on 20 August 1747 for 120 acres on Stith's Creek in the part of Brunswick County which became Lunenburg County in 1748 and Mecklenburg County in 1765 [Patents 28:135].

He was taxable in Lunenburg County in the list of Lewis Deloney in 1748, taxable in the list of Field Jefferson in 1751 with his son Tom [Bell, Sunlight on the Southside, 68, 166] and taxable with Thomas and Major Evans in 1752 [Tax List 1748-52, 1]. He petitioned the Lunenburg County court in May 1753 to be exempt from personal taxes, but was rejected "for Reasons appearing to the Court" [Orders 1753-54, 113].

He was granted 38 acres in Lunenburg County in the fork of Miles Creek and Dockery's Creek on 23 July 1753 [Patents 31:337]. He left a 22 March 1760 Brunswick County, Virginia will (signing), proved 27 October 1760, leaving his "Mannor" plantation on the south side of Dockery's Creek to his son Major Evans, left an equal quantity to his son Charles Evans and left the residue of his land on the southside of Dockery's Creek to son Dick Evans on condition they give twenty pounds or 100 acres of land to his youngest son Erasmus.

He left a bed and furniture to his daughters Sarah and Joice, but left only a shilling to his "undutiful" son Thomas

[WB 3:375-6]. He died before June 1760 when a suit against him in Lunenburg County court abated by his death [Orders 1759-61, 136]. On 18 October 1764 Sarah and Richard Evans sold about 39 acres in the fork of Miles and Dockery's Creek in Mecklenburg County which was land they had been given by Charles Evans [DB 1:514]. And on the same date Sarah, Charles and Major Evans sold 120 acres on Stith's Creek in Lunenburg County adjoining Philip Morgan.

His children were:

i. Thomas, born say 1734
ii. Major, born say 1735
iii. Charles, born say 1737
iv. Richard, born say 1740
v. Sarah Evans-(Pinn)
vi. Joyce
vii. Erasmus, born say 1745

Charles Evans was listed as a "yellow" complexioned soldier, born in Petersburg and living in Mecklenburg County when he enlisted in the Revolution [NSDAR, African American Patriots, 149].

Rawley Pinn was a "Mulatto" taxable in Buckingham County in 1774 [Woodson, Virginia Tithables From Burned Counties], head of an Amherst County household of 7 persons in 1783 [VA:47], and 8 "Mulattos" in 1785 [VA:84]. He was a free man of color who served in the Revolutionary War from Amherst County [NSDAR, African American Patriots, 152].

John Redcross was a soldier in the Revolutionary War from York County [Jackson, Virginia Negro Soldiers, 42]. He was taxable in York County in 1784 [Fothergill, Virginia Tax Payers, 103] and a "Mulatto" taxable on himself and a horse in Hanover County in 1785 and 1786.Cocke, Hanover County Taxpayers, St. Paul's Parish, 105.[52]

My ancestor, Robert Pinn IV, was the Grandson of Rawley and Sarah Pinn's son, James Pinn, and his second wife, Jane (Jinsey), Cooper-Powell Pinn. He was born in Amherst County Virginia (about 1817), to James and Jane Cooper Powell-Pinn. Their were two other children, Christina, and George Washington-Lafayette Pinn. It appears that there was enough knowledge of Washington and Lafayette for a son to receive their name. Rawley and Sarah had several other children, including Anna Pinn-(married Thomas Evans), Edy Pinn-(married William Beverly), Turner Pinn (married Joice Humbles).

There is more information about the Pinn family, in my first book, Notes And Documents of Free Persons of Color.

⌘ ⌘ ⌘

CHAPTER TWELVE

⁂ ⁂

RESEARCH AND THE RESEARCHER

"The history of a family over many generations lies buried in different sources and places. Like a good detective, the genealogist must search for the pieces of a family's past in those many sources such as books, documents, and manuscripts. The genealogist must also be patient and imaginative, for the search can take years and involve a string of clues that lead to new sources. The facts—names, dates, events—that a genealogist gathers through the years are like pieces of a puzzle. Gradually those pieces can be fitted together to make a picture of a family, its many members, and its unique history."[53]

Genealogy is the study and tracing of your family lineage. It involves collecting the names of relatives, both living and deceased, and establishing the relationships between them based on primary, secondary and/or circumstantial evidence or documentation, thus building a cohesive Family Tree. Genealogy is sometimes referred to as family history, although it is the study of your family lines. Your family history may include historical data about family origins, and other historical information.

It is one of the most fascinating, and rewarding pastimes, you can engage in, and so is tracing your family history. By delving into the past of your family and the families that have joined together to form that family, you can learn about yourself, your parents, your ancestors, and the many people who have been born, wedded, had children, and eventually ended up creating that unique entity known as you. As well, you can learn much about what those people did and the places from which they came.

In A family history, you will create a profile of your family's journey from the past to the present. Researching your genealogy is important in terms of social organization, especially where people lived and worked, and their day to day lives. Marriage Unions are also looked at in the context of the differing racial groups. European, African, Asian, and Native marriage ceremonies differed in many aspects.

Once you have a list of names, the real search begins. You need to find as much information about these people as possible. Many of us have oral family histories that can be utilized. The oral family history contains important information, names, dates, and events that can be used in your search. Once you have the oral history written down, find documentation of the names, and other information. This is where public records, such as census, wills, school records; birth and death certificates come in handy. Legal papers can be a wealth of information about the people from whom you are descended. Such items as deeds, real estate papers, and loan papers can tell you a great deal about the names on your family tree.

SURMOUNTABLE BRICK WALLS

Genealogical research can be quite rewarding, once those annoying Brick Walls are removed. The task of finding multi-racial ancestry complicates the search even further. You may begin looking at an African American Ancestor, and then find there is a branch that is White or Native. Do you add that branch to your family tree? Well it depends, on how close they are, or if it will add something to the existing history. I have several ancestors whose line leads to Europeans, and to Natives. Some of the lines are more connected than others, and are already known to family members.

The entire search will take a new direction as you follow your clues. This is especially tricky in the south where racial divides were more pronounced. In my case my ancestors, who were free prior to the Civil War, were often categorized in several racial categories. They could be white, mulatto, and then Negro within their lifetime. It was according to what the laws were regarding the classification of race. Those laws were written largely by white males, especially in the south. This was the situation with my Mulatto ancestors, in Colonial Virginia.

There is a bias amongst those who believe that there was little or no interaction between Indians and Blacks. It is difficult for some to separate the prejudices they have today, from our countries history. Since my family was Native/White/African, it has been a matter of separating and tracing those lines individually. In order to have a fruitful search it was imperative to trace the lines as far back as I could.

During my initial search, I often ran into brick walls that seemed insurmountable, but the key was knowing the answers to, who, what, and where. Who I was looking for, what information was available, and where was the information located. This meant finding which City, County, State, and Time Period the ancestor lived in. Then there was the racial identity question; in other words, what race did they identify with.

During the, Trail of Tears, there were not many Natives, listing themselves (in Federal Census records) as, Indian, and for good reason. During the mid to late 1800's, they were being shipped to reservations, in the west. The ones who did not want to be removed blended into the communities they lived in. This is the same period that the Free Blacks were leaving and resetting in Nova Scotia, Canada and/or Liberia. This was the cleansing time, moving people around, as Europeans seeking freedom came into America. This is not a pleasant truth, but history is not always pleasant.

"Many Native Americans accepted baptism, the act of which, in the view of Christian society, converted them participants from 'heathens' or 'savages' to Christians. The simple act of baptism kept them from being swept up in Jacksonian , permitting them to live on the margins of transplanted European-derived society.

The implications for the historical record were ominous. In effect, baptism brought about a change of status, from persons with Native American Heritage to an officially recorded racial class of 'colored' or 'mulatto' or 'black'. The result of this process of virtual "Pleckerization" was a population of Native-descended people in Delaware whose recorded history became inseparable from colored persons of other ethnic derivations."[54]

It should also be noted that the lighter skinned Native Americans were able to assimilate (if they desired), as white. Many Natives were able to gain, "Honorary White Status," and blend into the dominant society. This is not an indictment against Natives who were facing genocide, and doing what was necessary to continue to survive.

SOME STEPS TO TAKE

1. Survey the field to see what has already been done.. Whether researching the history of a house, a military unit, a family, or a town, it is essential to see if the subject has already been researched. The holdings of libraries and archives, many of which are now on-line, should be consulted as should the book reviews in journals and the publishers' catalogs (many of which are now also on line).
2. Contact as many living relatives as possible.. Find out what they know or suspect. Ask them to be as specific as possible as to names, dates, and places. When anyone tells you anything, write down who told you, and the date the conversation was held.
3. Search for any family papers. They might be in the attic, the basement, or a safe-deposit box. Family Bibles, letters, diaries, insurance policies: any documents left by family members may be helpful.
4. Plan trips to library or archives. There are a number of research facilities you may wish to visit. You can find government records your State Archives. Other libraries have family and private records.

5. Before visiting any libraries or archives, analyze exactly what objectives need to be achieved.
6. For each problem, keep a research calendar. At the top of the page state your objective and then list every place you looked, whether you found anything or not. Include the date you searched.

RESEARCHING YOUR SURNAMES

Are you one of the Millions of Smith, or Jones out there? Take heart, it is not an impossible task to trace your name. The key is where these surnames were and when they were there. Start by doing an Internet Search and find a list for the State, City, and county where your ancestors lived. You can also do a search on the history of the surname, and its meaning. For instance, my maiden name is Baxter, which is Anglo-Saxon, and also Bagster, or Baker.

This information was not surprising since the surname belonged to the person who owned my ancestors in South Carolina. You may be surprised with the kind of information you will unearth when you do research on your own family name. People you've never known existed, long-lost relatives, and friends who share the same lineage as you! This is what researching your own surname can do for you. If you're not ready for some surprise findings, you're better off leaving all this researching to others in your family.

Researching your own surname can be done through different methods the most popular among all of the other of researching your family surname is through the Internet. You can reach out anywhere in the world, and find information. The wide availability, freedom of use and flexibility of the internet makes it a popular genealogical research tool.

Rootsweb is a popular site on the internet, as is Cyndi's list. Another popular sites is Ancestry.com, although there is a fee. There are also many free sites, on the web, that you should check out. Also join a list such as Virginia History List (or whatever state, or County you are researching), where others who are researching your area are posting, and post a query. You can also check out Family History Centers, which are in most communities. These centers are operated by the Mormon Church, and have been very helpful to me in my search.

By typing in your surname or your ancestor's first and last name, you will come up with a whole list of possible family members that you can easily fill up your family tree. These tools are generally easy to use and some websites even have communication tools whereby you can contact the possible relative directly too. These websites contain hundreds of millions of family names in their database to help people find long-lost family members.

You can begin your search right in your own home. Start with the person that you know best, yourself. Write down your name, your date and place of birth and your date and place of marriage. Next, record the following information about your parents: their names (always use a wife's maiden name), date and place of birth, date and place of marriage, date and place of death, and place of burial. Now do the same with your grandparents. You now have three generations to work with. Continue to go back as far as you can. After finishing, record all this information on your pedigree chart.

Now get in touch with your relatives: parents, grandparents, aunts and uncles. Contact the oldest first. If you are fortunate enough to be able to interview them in person, bring along your pedigree charts and family group sheets so that you will know what information you are lacking. Gather all the information from them that you can. Take notes, or better yet, use a tape recorder if you have one.

If your relatives are distant, contact them by letter. Type or print clearly. Inform them of your intent and supply them with a list of specific questions. Be brief and enclose a stamped, self-addressed envelope. Also consider visiting or writing old friends of the family as they may also be able to supply you with valuable information.

In your family history, you can create a profile of your family's journey from the past to the present. Researching your genealogy is important in terms of social organization, especially where people lived and worked, and their day to day lives. Marriage Unions are also looked at in the context of the differing racial groups. European, Hispanic, African, Asian, and Native marriage ceremonies differed in many aspects.

Genealogical research requires as much care and diligence as any other research project. It is vitally important, therefore, to start out with a definite plan for arranging and filing the material that you gather. It is also important to remember that in genealogical research you will find a great number of apparently unrelated facts and items. An item here and an item there may seem to have no connection, and yet a third item may link it all together. Such a happy combination is impossible if, through bad organization, the first two were not accessible when you found the third.

Once you have figured out names, the real digging begins. You need to find as much information about these people as possible. Anything in the public record is usually the best place to start. Legal papers can be a wealth of information about the people from whom you are descended. Such items as deeds, real estate papers, and loan papers can tell you a great deal about the names on your family tree. This is the meat of any family history, and with a few details, you can begin filling in a whole lot of blanks.

The task of finding multi-racial ancestry complicates the genealogical search even further. You may begin looking at an African American Ancestor, and then find that there was a white parent, or a Native parent. The entire search will take a new direction as you follow your clues. People who decide to trace their family histories may know next to nothing about their family, and need to begin researching from scratch. Then there are those who already have a good knowledge about their family, but need to document it properly and fill in some blanks. In both instances, the records reviewed may be about the same, but it may be more intense for people in the first situation.

When you are researching, you will be the judge of the materials at your disposal. You are entitled to your opinion, especially after you do the research. Don't lose sight of your search, and what you are trying to accomplish. Sometimes you will find stories that were not told in history books, and it is up to you whether to put it publish it.

If your relatives live far away, call, email (if possible), or contact them by letter. Ask specific questions, requesting names, dates and places; and take notes. If you write a letter, Type or print clearly. Be brief and enclose a stamped, self-addressed envelope. Also consider visiting or writing old friends of the family as they may be able to supply you with valuable information.

ITEMS YOU WILL NEED:

LOOSE-LEAF NOTEBOOK

One eight-and-a-half by eleven inches in size is preferable because it is not only convenient to carry, but you can insert and rearrange all your correspondence, typewritten papers, Photostats and other valuable notes and papers with a minimum of trouble.

Files and a filing system, to store and manage documents.

A smaller pocket size Notebook for jotting down notes and information when traveling.

PENCILS AND PAPER, AND INK PENS

A Pencil is all right for temporary notes, but eventually, smudging will result in loss of legibility or even in complete obliteration. Pen and ink make the ideal combination - wherever, of course, the library or institution will permit their use.

KEEPING RECORDS

It is important to keep an accurate record of all the source material that you consult. An eight-and-one-half inch loose leaf notebook will work well here also. Fill it with lined paper. I used Index cards to write down the individual surnames and locations I searched. Write down the library call number, title, author, publisher, date of publication, page number, volume number, and any other related information.

PEDIGREE CHARTS AND FAMILY GROUP SHEETS

The Pedigree Chart and Family Group Sheet is invaluable aids for the Genealogist. The pedigree chart shows direct descent and does not include brothers and sisters. It shows direct lines of your parents, grandparents, and great grandparents. The family group sheet will record the children, if any, resulting from each marriage.

Along with the children's names, you may also record statistical information such as dates and places of birth, death, and marriage on the group sheet. Insert these records in your workbook. Many types of pedigree charts and family group sheets are available. Pedigree Charts range from elaborate fan shapes designed for as many as ten generations to simple bracketed charts for five generations.

There are various patented devices for holding notes, or for preserving family records, which are obtainable at bookstores, which specialize in genealogical publications. The old-fashioned Family Tree with its trunk, branches, and twigs periodically falls in and out of favor but is, nevertheless, an interesting way to display your lineage.

HISTORY SHEETS

Use History Sheets to record supplementary information about your ancestors such as anecdotes, newspaper accounts, or any other miscellaneous historical information you may uncover. This type of information will add color and depth to your family history.

The two basic classifications of sources from which you will obtain your genealogical information are Primary and Secondary:

1. Primary sources consist of authentic, original records such as land deeds, birth and death certificates, wills, marriage certificates, or photocopies of original documents and official government records.
2. Secondary sources consist of family oral traditions, records later copied or transcribed (there may be errors) and any other information recorded sometime after the fact: the longer afterward, the less reliable. Published Family Histories are secondary sources and should not be taken for fact as they are often inaccurate. However do not discount secondary sources altogether. They will often provide

valuable clues and you can include them on your history sheet. Sometimes they may be the only information that you have about a particular ancestor.

When I started in 1978, there was no internet with information at my fingertips. Back then, the preferred methods of contact were phone calls, and/or writing letters. The libraries were just starting to stock general genealogical information. This was of necessity, since I lived in California and almost all of information was on the East Coast. A pencil and notepad will come in handy when you are asking questions. Make sure to write down, names, addresses, and other pertinent information.

Go back over the chapter and make notes, before beginning your research project. You want to have a map of where you are and where you are going, before starting. Once you beginning talking to people, and communicating by whatever means, you want to begin your journal. When documents start arriving, file them in a safe place, where they can be easily located. This is the beginning of your family history, and the first step in your journey.

Researching your own surname can be done through different methods being through the Internet. If you do not have access to a computer, most libraries or Family History Centers, will allow you access. There are Computer labs in Community Colleges, and Universities that may grant you time to do research. You can also join a local historical, or genealogy society, and meet others who are researching. You can reach out anywhere in the world, and find information. The wide availability, freedom of use and flexibility of the internet makes it a popular genealogical research tool.

One of the most popular sites is Ancestry.com, although there is a fee. There are also many free sites, on the web, that you should check out. Cyndi's List is an excellent resource referral site to those who need specific directions. Also join a list such as Virginia History list, or Virginia Roots (or whatever state, or County you are researching), where others who are researching your area can and will assist you.

With some sites it is as simple as typing in your surname or your ancestor's first and last name. You will then come up with a whole list of possible family members that can easily fill up your family tree. These tools are generally easy to use and some websites even have communication tools whereby you can contact the possible relative directly too. These websites contain hundreds of millions of family names in their database to help people find long-lost family members.

You can begin the search in your own home. Start with your immediate family, with yourself as the first person. You will be doing an Ancestry Chart, beginning with yourself, then your parents, grandparents, and so forth. Write down your name, date and place of birth and and your biographical information. Next, record the following information about your parents: their names (always use a wife's maiden name), date and place of birth, date and place of marriage, date and place of death, and place of burial. Now do the same with your grandparents. You now have three generations to work with. Continue to go back as far as you can. After finishing, record all this information on your pedigree chart.

Example: BAXTER, George (born Orangeburg South Carolina, May 27, 1918), married MARTIN, Vivian (born Coatesville Pennsylvania, January 28, 1923), Cecil County Maryland, February 10, 1940.

Now get in touch with your relatives: parents, grandparents, aunts and uncles. Contact the oldest first. If you are fortunate enough to be able to interview them in person, bring along your Pedigree Charts and Family Group Sheets so that you will know what information you are lacking. Gather all the information from them that you can. Take notes, or better yet, use a tape recorder if you have one.

If your relatives are are at a distance, contact them by letter. Type or print clearly and inform them of your intent, before supplying them with a list of specific questions. Be brief and enclose a stamped, self-addressed envelope. Also, consider visiting or writing old friends of the family as they may also be able to supply you with valuable information.

Things to keep in mind when interviewing or writing for information

- Make your questions specific. You will have a better chance of getting an answer. If you ask general questions, your correspondence may yield no results. Older relatives may need specific questions to have their memories jogged. Ask about specific people, specific times, and specific places.
- Inquire about photographs, diaries, letters and other family papers that may yield clues. Look for items such as obituaries, birth announcements or marriage records, and birth or death certificates. You will find older copies of documents through Newspaper Archives, Department of Vital Statistics, or through your County Historical Society.
- Keep track of what you are told in a carefully dated and documented fashion. A loose-leaf notebook, and file cards are enough at first. Write down who told you what, for each piece of information. If a relative sends you an undated letter, make a note of the date you received it. If you use a tape recorder, begin the tape with the date and location and the name of the person you are interviewing, as well as your own name.

When I started, my method of contact was phone calls, or writing letters. In those pre-internet days Phone calls were necessary to make contacts with relatives, and check potential sources for information. I kept a pencil and notepad to write down names and pertinent information. I still have the original notes written during those interviews.

⌘ ⌘ ⌘

CHAPTER THIRTEEN

✼ ✼

A BEGINNER'S GUIDE TO DNA AND GENEALOGY

There is quite a bit of information on DNA (Deoxyribonucleic Acid), on the internet and in Libraries. I am not an expert on DNA, and you do not have to be an expert to have a sample taken. One drop of spit contains cells that can lead back thousands of years. My brother, myself, and several other relatives, have had DNA tests. The labs are as diverse as the African Ancestry Project, Family Tree DNA, and National Geographic Genographics Lab. My Maternal female line is European, my brother's paternal male line test, is Native American, and our maternal Grandmother's line is from Northern Nigeria. Now how is that for diversity?

AFRICA'S SEVEN DAUGHTERS OF EVE (MITOCHONDRIAL EVE)

According to Family Tree DNA, research over the last decade has suggested several maternal lines ultimately all originating from the first woman "Eve" approximately 140,000 years ago in Africa.

- The clan of Ursula left Africa about 45,000 years ago by the first modern humans, Homo sapiens, as they established themselves in Europe. Today, about 11% of modern Europeans are the direct maternal descendants of Ursula. They come from all parts of Europe, but the clan is well represented in western Britain and Scandinavia.

- <u>The clan of Xenia</u> was founded 25,000 years ago by the second wave of modern humans, Homo sapiens, who established themselves in Europe, just prior to the coldest part of the last Ice Age. Today around 7% of native Europeans are in the clan of Xenia. Within the clan, three distinct branches fan out over Europe. One is still largely confined to Eastern Europe while the other two have spread further to the West into central Europe and as far as France and Britain. About 1% of Native Americans are also in the clan of Xenia.

- <u>The clan of Helena</u> began about 20,000 years ago with the birth of Helena somewhere in the valleys of the Dordogne and the Veered, in south-central France. The clan is widespread throughout all parts of Europe, but reaches its highest frequency among the Basque people of northern Spain and southern France.

- <u>The clan of Veda</u> (Scandinavian for ruler) is the smallest of the seven clans containing only about 4% of native Europeans. Velda lived 17,000 years ago in the limestone hills of Cantabria in northwest Spain. Her descendants are found nowadays mainly in western and northern Europe and are surprisingly frequent among the Saami people of Finland and Northern Norway.

- <u>The clan of Tara</u> (Gaelic for rocky hill) includes slightly fewer than 10% of modern Europeans. Its many branches are widely distributed throughout southern and western Europe with particularly high concentrations in Ireland and the west of Britain. Tara herself lived 17,000 years ago in the northwest of Italy among the hills of Tuscany and along the estuary of the river Arno.

- <u>The clan of Katrine</u> (Greek for pure) is a medium sized clan with 10% of Europeans among its membership. Katrine herself lived 15,000 years ago in the wooded plains of northeast Italy, now flooded by the Adriatic, and among the southern foothills of the Alps. Her descendants are still there in numbers, but have also spread throughout central and northern Europe.

- The clan of Jasmine (Persian for flower) is the second largest of the seven European clans after Helena and is the only one to have its origins outside Europe. Jasmine and her descendants, who now make up 12% of Europeans, were among the first farmers and brought the agricultural revolution to Europe from the Middle East around 8,500 years ago.

That DNA test took my maternal line through Virginia, into Wales, through Switzerland, Germany, Russia, Spain, and North Africa. My female ancestor traversed from North Africa, and into the Basque Region of Spain. She would have been traveling with her clan or tribe, and her DNA is still found in those areas. However, my ancestor left that region and started traveling throughout Europe. The mapping of my DNA traces the areas where those ancestors settled.

I communicated with a DNA cousin from Belrusia, who stated that many were scattered from the Basque Region of Spain during the Spanish Inquisition.

SOME DNA DEFINITIONS

- Allele: One of the variant forms of a gene at a particular locus, or location, on a chromosome. Different alleles produce variation in inherited characteristics. For STR markers, each allele is the number of repeats of the short base sequence.
- Base Pair: Two bases that form a "rung of the DNA ladder." A DNA nucleotide is made of a molecule of sugar, a molecule of phosphoric acid, and a molecule called a base. The bases are the "letters" that spell out the genetic code. In DNA, the code letters are A, T, G, and C, which stand for the chemicals adenine, thymine, guanine, and cytosine, respectively. In base pairing, adenine always pairs with thymine, and guanine always pairs with cytosine.
- Chromosome: One of the threadlike "packages" of genes and other DNA in the nucleus of a cell.

- DYS#: D=DNA, Y=Y chromosome, S=a unique DNA segment. A label for genetic markers on the Y chromosome. Each marker is designated by a number, according to international conventions. At present, virtually all the DYS designations are given to STR markers (a class often used in genetic genealogy).
- Gene: The functional and physical unit of heredity passed from parent to offspring. Genes are pieces of DNA, and most genes contain the information for making a specific protein.
- Genome: The entire DNA contained in an organism or a cell, which includes both the chromosomes within the nucleus and the DNA in mitochondria.
- Locus: A point in the genome, identified by a marker, which can be mapped by some means. It does not necessarily correspond to a gene. A single gene may have several loci within it (each defined by different markers) and these markers may be separated in genetic or physical mapping experiments. In such cases, it is useful to define these different loci, but normally the gene name should be used to designate the gene itself, as this usually will convey the most information.
- Marker: Also known as a genetic marker, a segment of DNA with an identifiable physical location on a chromosome whose inheritance can be followed. A marker can be a gene, or it can be some section of DNA with no known function. Because DNA segments that lie near each other on a chromosome tend to be inherited together, markers are often used as indirect ways of tracking the inheritance pattern of genes that have not yet been identified, but whose approximate locations are known.
- Micro satellite: Repetitive stretches of short sequences of DNA used as genetic markers to track inheritance in families.
- Mutation: A permanent structural alteration in DNA.
- Short Tandem Repeats (STR): A genetic marker consisting of multiple copies of an identical DNA sequence arranged in direct succession in a particular region of a chromosome. Occasionally, one

⌘ ⌘ ⌘

APPENDIX

⸗ ⸗

RACIAL CLASSIFICATIONS IN THE AMERICAN CENSUS

Racial classifications have appeared on every US census, from America's first census in 1790. Although the term 'color' was used in nineteenth-century American censuses, it was synonymous with 'race'.

Following are the Four Periods of the American Census:

The first period is 1790–1840

The second period is 1850–1920

The third period is 1930–1960

The fourth period is 1970–2000

The 1970 census was the first after the formal dissolution of the Civil Rights movement and the first for which self-identification (as opposed to enumerator identification) was uniformly used.

1850–1920

The 1850 census changed US census taking in many ways. A large part of its significance rests in the introduction of the "Mulatto" category and the reasons for its introduction. It was not added because of demographic shifts; rather, it was added because of the lobbying efforts of a prominent racial scientist of the US Senate and the willingness of certain senators to do his biding (Nobles 2000: 35-43). By the 1850s, polygenic thought was winning a battle that it was losing in Europe.

The 'American School of Ethnology' distinguished itself from prevailing European racial thought by its tenet that human races were distinct and unequal species. There was, however, considerable resistance initially to polygenic. Although most American monogeneses were not racial egalitarians, they were unwilling to accept claims of separate origins, permanent racial differences, and the infertility of racially mixed persons. Polygenesis deliberately sought hard statistical data to prove that mulattos, as hybrids of different racial species, were less fertile than their parents of pure races were and hence lived shorter lives.

Racial theorist, medical doctor, scientist, and slave-owner Josiah Nott purposefully lobbied certain senators for the inclusion of several inquiries on the census, all designed to prove his theory of mulatto hybrids and separate origins.

Negroes-A persons of mixed white and Negro blood should be returned as a Negro, no matter how small the percentage of Negro blood. Both black and mulatto persons are to be returned as Negroes, without distinction. A person of mixed Indian and Nero blood should be returned a Negro, unless the Indian blood predominates and the status of an Indian is generally accepted in the community. Indians-A persons of mixed white and Indian blood should be returned as Indian, except where the percentage of Indian blood is very small, or where those in the community regard he/she as a white person where he/she lives.

Other mixed races-Any mixture of white and non-white should be reported according to the non-white parent. Mixtures of colored races should be reported according to the non-white parent. Mixtures of colored races should be reported according to the race of the father, except Negro-Indian (see definition of Negro).

The Civil Rights Movement and resultant civil rights legislation of the 1960 has dramatically changed the political context of census taking. That political context had been one of the bold stratification of privileges and penalties along racial lines in virtually all aspects of American public life. Laws spelled out the boundaries of racial membership; institutional mechanisms and social customs reinforced them. It included a context in which the process of racial categorization in the census had been largely out of public view. Politicians, (social) scientists, and later Bureau officials decided on race categories with little public attention, input or accountability. Enumerators categorized persons by observation, according to the instructions provided to them.

1930–1960

With the permanent elimination of 'mulatto', US census categorization came in line with southern race laws and the 'one-drop' rule of black racial membership. According to the rule, 'one-drop of black blood' made persons black and conferred all of the legal, social political and economic disabilities associated with the designation. As importantly, race laws codified 'white racial purity' according to which one was either purely white or one was not.

Blood droplets were literally the standard and these standards guided federal census by 1930. Enumerator instructions for the 1930–1950 censuses explicitly used terminology of blood in their definition of Negroes and Indians. It is notable that Enumerator's instructions have never included a definition of' white; however, 'Japanese', Filipino, 'Hindu', and 'Korean', were included under, the 1930 and 1940 schedules enumerators, and given no racial definition. The 1960 census defined 'negro' without an explicit reference to 'blood quanta' at all. However, any person having at least one 'Negro' parent was to be classified as Negro.[55]

⌘ ⌘ ⌘

GLOSSARY OF
GENEALOGICAL TERMS

≠ ≠

A

Abolition Movement: From the 1830s, until the Civil War, the abolitionists working in the abolition movement sought to emancipate slaves and end slavery, also; abolitionism

Abstract: Abbreviated transcription of a document or record that includes the date of the record, every name appearing therein, the relationship (if stated) of each person named and their description (ie. witness, executor, bondsman, son, widow, etc.), and if they signed with their signature or mark.

Accordant (with): Agreeing

Acre: A unit of area in the U.S. Customary System, used in land and sea floor measurement and equal to 160 square rods, 4,840 square yards, or 43,560 square feet.

ACRG (American Cross-Race Gen): Website devoted to researching cross-racial American family history and/or ancestors who were or may have been of mixed-race ancestry, at http://www.rootsweb. com/~genrace/genrace.index.htm?sourceid=0038878616720684 0432.

ACS: See American Colonization Society

Ad litem: Legal term meaning in this case only. For example, "George Thomas, duly appointed by the court, may administer ad litem the settlement of the estate of Joseph Thomas, deceased."

admin. (abbreviation): Administrator, administration.

Administration: Management and settlement of an estate.

Administrator: An appointee of the court who settles the estate of a deceased person who died without leaving a will.

Administratrix: A female Administrator.

admon. (abbreviation): Letters of administration.

Affidavit: a written or oral statement made under oath.

Africa: The second-largest continent, lying south of Europe between the Atlantic and Indian oceans. Africa has vast mineral resources, many of which are still undeveloped.

African: A native or inhabitant of Africa. According to all available data the ancestors of Modern man originated in Africa.

AG: The International Commission for the Accreditation of Professional Genealogists, internationally recognized as ICAPGenSM, administers the Accreditation Program.

Agnate: Ones genetic relative exclusively through males; a kinsman with whom one has a common ancestor by descent in unbroken male line.

Ahnentafel: Ancestor table tabulates the ancestry of one individual by generation in text rather than pedigree chart format. A comprehensive ahnentafel gives more than the individual's name, date and place of birth, christening, marriage, death and burial. It should give biographical and historical commentary for each person listed, as well as footnotes citing the source documents used to prove what is stated.

Ahnentafel Number: The unique number assigned to each position in an ancestor table is called an ahnentafel number. Number one designates the person in the first generation. Numbers two and three designate the parents of number one and the second generation. Numbers four through seven designate the grandparents of person number one and the third generation. As the ahnentafel extends by generation, the number of persons doubles.

a.k.a.: Also known as; alias.

ALARS: American Library Association Records Standards

Alien: A citizen of another country.

American Colonization Society (ACS): Established in 1816 by Robert Finley, with the intent of settling Freed Blacks in Africa.

American Revolution: U.S. War for Independence from Great Britain 1775–1783

Ancestor: Any person from whom one is descended, especially one earlier in a family line than a grandparent; forefather; forebear.

Ancestor Chart: Report or chart that shows a person and all of their ancestors in a graphical format.

Ancestral File: A computerized file of individual and family records, created from records and pedigree charts submitted to the Family History Department of the Church of Jesus Christ of Latter-day Saints since 1979. The purpose of the Ancestral File is to help people coordinate their research.

Ancestry: Denotes all of your ancestors from your parents as far back as they are traceable. Estimates suggest that everyone has approximately 65,000 traceable ancestors, meaning ancestors whose existence can be documented in surviving records.

Anglo-Saxon: The Anglos and Saxons invaded and settled in Britain in the 5th century.

Annotation: Many types of genealogical presentations contain statements, record sources, documents, conclusions, or other historical information that require an annotation. Genealogists use annotations to explain discrepancies between two or more documents, to add information from another source to support a statement or conclusion made in a different record, and other difficult to interpret situations.

anon. (abbreviation): Anonymous.

Ante: Latin prefix meaning before, such as in ante-bellum South, "The South before the war"

APG: Association of Professional Genealogists (APG), members promote genealogy as a profession and encourage professionalism in genealogy.

appr. (abbreviation): Appraisal; appraisement.

Apprentice: One bound by indenture to serve another for a prescribed period with a view to learning an art or trade. One who is learning by practical experience under skilled workers a trade, art, or calling

Appurtenance: That which belongs to something else such as a building, orchard, right of way, etc.

Archive: Collection of public or corporate records; place where such records are kept.

Ascendants: Lineal Ancestors.

Asia: The world's largest continent. It occupies the eastern part of the Eurasian landmass and its adjacent islands and is separated from Europe by the Ural Mountains.

Asian: Denoting or characteristic of the bio geographic region including southern Asia and the Malay Archipelago as far as the Philippines and Borneo and Java.

Assignment: Grant of property or a legal right, benefit, or privilege to another person.

Attest: To affirm; to certify by signature of oath.

Authenticate: Prove a document is not a forgery.

B

b. (abbreviation): born.

Bamako: The capital and largest city of Mali, in the southwest on the Niger River. It was a leading center of Muslim learning under the Mali Empire (c. 11th-15th centuries).

BANNS: Public announcement of intended marriage.

Banns: Public announcement of an intended marriage, generally made in church.

bapt. (abbreviation): baptized

Baptism: The ceremony or sacrament of admitting a person into Christianity or a specific Christian church by dipping the person in water or pouring or sprinkling water on them;

Baptismal Certificate: A formal document normally kept by a church of baptisms that occurred in their congregation. It typically contains the names of the individuals baptized, the date of baptism, where it took place, the clergyman's name, and possibly the names of sponsors and place of residence.

Base-born: child born to unmarried parents

Bastard: Child born outside of marriage.

BCG: Board for Certification of Genealogists, P.O. Box 14291, Washington, DC 20044 (USA and international). Genealogists certified by the BCG must renew their certification every five years, through a renewal examination process.

bef. (abbreviation): Before.

Beneficiary: One who receives benefit of trust or property.

Bequeath: Term appearing in a will meaning to leave or give property as specified therein to another person or organization.

Bequest: Legacy; usually a gift of real estate by will.

Berber: A member of a North African, primarily Muslim people living in settled or nomadic tribes from Morocco to Egypt. Any of the Afro-Asiatic languages of the Berbers.

bet. (abbreviation): Between

Bibliography: List of writings relating to a specific subject, some of which are annotated. A bibliographic citation describes and identifies the author, edition, date of issue, publisher, and typography of a book or other written material.

Biographer: The author of a biography.

Biographies: A biography is a book written about a particular individual. You can also find compiled biographies, which are books that contain short biographies of many different people. A compiled biography normally is about a specific group of people.

Biography: The history of a person's life

Birth Certificate: A formal document normally issued by a government body responsible for the registration of vital statistics within a particular jurisdiction

Birth records: A birth record contains information about the birth of an individual. On a birth record, you can usually find the mother's full maiden name and the father's full name, the name of the baby, the date of the birth, and county where the birth took place. Many birth records include other information, such as the birthplaces of the baby's parents, the addresses of the parents, the number of children that the parents have, and the race of the parents, and the parents' occupations.

Black Dutch: Sephardic Jews who married Dutch protestants to escape the Inquisition, many of their descendants later moving to the Americas, the "black" referring to their dark hair and complexion; Descendents of marriages between Dutch women and Portuguese soldiers stationed in the Netherlands as part of Spanish forces in the Spanish-Dutch wars 1555–1609. See also Melungeons.

Black Irish: The Black Irish are a population group in Ireland possessing dark skin and hair, purportedly due to Iberian ancestry.

Bond: Written, binding agreement to perform as specified. Many types of bonds have existed for centuries and appear in marriage, land and court records used by genealogists. Historically, laws required administrators and executors of estates, grooms alone or with others, and guardians of minors to post bonds. It is not unusual to discover that a bondsman was related to someone involved in the action before the court. If a bondsman failed to perform, the court may have demanded payment of a specified sum as a penalty.

Bondsman: Person acting as surety for a bond (often, but by no means ordinarily, a relative).

Bond Written: Signed, witnessed agreement requiring payment of a specified amount of money on or before a given date.

Border: A small-holder, usually on the outskirts of a town.

Bounds: Pertaining to measuring natural or man-made features on the land.

Bounty land: Land promised as an inducement for enlistment or payment for military services. A central government did not exist when the Revolutionary War began, nor did a treasury. Land, the greatest asset the new nation possessed, was used to induce enlistment and as payment for military services. Those authorized to bounty land received a Bounty Land Warrant from the newly formed government after the war.

Bounty Land Warrant: A right to obtain land, specific number of acres of unallocated public land, granted for military service.

bp. (abbreviation): Baptized.

bpt. (abbreviation): Baptized.

bro. (abbreviation): Brother.

bu. (abbreviation): Buried.

Buffalo soldier: A member of one of the African-American regiments within the U.S. Army after the Civil War, serving primarily in the Indian wars of the late 1860s.

bur. (abbreviation): Buried.

Burial record: A formal account normally kept by a church of burials that occurred in their congregation. Besides the names of the deceased, it may contain the age of the person at death, their birth date, and cause of death, the clergyman's name, and possibly the place of residence at the time of death.

Buried Partly: Indicates the heart is buried in one place and the body in another, usually by directions of a will.

C

c., ca.: (abbreviation): About or around, (also see circa).

CAILS: Certified American Indian Lineage Specialist, BCG credential

CALS: Certified American Lineage Specialist, BCG credential.

Canon law: Church law.

Cascading Pedigree Chart: A series of Pedigree Charts that span multiple generations for an individual.

cem. (abbreviation): Cemetery.

Cemetery record: An account of the names and death dates of those buried within a cemetery.

Census: Official enumeration, listing or counting of citizens.

Census Record: A government sponsored enumeration of the population in a particular area; contains a variety of information from names heads of household or all household members, their ages, citizenship status, and ethnic background etc.

Census: Official enumeration, listing or counting of citizens.

Certified Copy: A copy made and attested to by officers having charge of the original and authorized to give copies.

Certify: To confirm formally as true, accurate, or genuine. To guarantee as meeting a standard.

CG: Certified Genealogist, BCG credential.

CG©: Certified Genealogist (Canada), see also Genealogical Institute of the Maritimes.

CGI: Certified Genealogical Instructor, BCG credential.

CGL: Certified Genealogical Lecturer, BCG credential.

CGRS: Certified Genealogical Record Specialist, BCG credential.

Chain: 100 links; 66 feet.

Chattel: Any property other than freehold land, including tangible goods (chattels personal), and leasehold interested (Chattels Real).

Cherokee: A Native American people formerly inhabiting the southern Appalachian Mountains from the western Carolinas and eastern Tennessee to northern Georgia, with present-day populations in northeast Oklahoma and western North Carolina. The Cherokee were removed to Indian Territory in the 1830s during the, "Trail of Tears." The Cherokee are part of the Iroquoian Linguistic group.

Cholera: Acute severe contagious diarrhea with intestinal lining sloughing.

chr. (abbreviation): Christened.

Christening: Christian ceremony of baptizing and giving a first name to an infant. See also baptism

Christian name: A first name given at Baptism, usually a first name from the Bible (Mary, Ruth, Joseph).

Church of Jesus Christ of Latter-day Saints: Christian religion founded in 1830 by Joseph Smith, the Mormons.

Church Records: Church records are the formal documents that churches have kept about their congregations through the years. Churches normally record information about christenings, baptisms, marriages, and burials. The types of information you will find in the records are the name(s) of the individual(s) involved, the date of the event, the location of the event, and the clergyman's name.

Circa: About, near, or approximate—usually referring to a date.

Citation: Pertinent information needed to find the full text of a publication. Citations are provided in bibliographies, indexes, and the lists of references in scholarly works. Citation of a book generally includes: author(s), title, publisher, date. Citation of an article in a periodical generally includes: author(s), article title, source journal title, volume, pages, and date.

Citizen: A member of a state; a native or naturalized person who owes allegiance to a government and is entitled to protection from it.

civ. (abbreviation): Civil

Civil law: Laws concerned with civil or private rights and remedies, as contrasted with criminal law; body of law established by a nation, commonwealth, county or city, also called municipal law.

Civil War: War Between the States: War between North and South (Union & Confederate Army's) 1861–1865.

Clan: A group comprising a number of households whose heads claim descent from a common ancestor (similar to tribe).

Codicil: Supplement or addition to a will; not intended to replace an entire will.

Colic: An abdominal pain and cramping.

Collateral Ancestor: An ancestor not in the direct line of ascent, but of the same ancestral family

Collateral Families: The families with whom your ancestors intermarried.

Collateral Line: Line of descent connecting persons who share a common ancestor, but are related through an aunt, uncle, cousin, nephew, etc.

comm. (abbreviation): Communion, communicant.

Common ancestor: Person through who two or more persons claim descent or lineage.

Communicant: Person receiving communion in a religious ceremony or service.

conf. (abbreviation): Confirmed.

Confederacy: Collectively the Confederate States of America; the Southern American States which succeeded from the United States in 1860–1861.

Confederate: Pertaining to the Southern states which seceded from theU.S. in 1860 –1861, their government and their citizens.

Congestion: Any collection of fluid in an organ, like the lungs.

Congestive chills: Malaria with diarrhea.

Congestive fever: Malaria.

Connubial: Of or relating to the married state; conjugal.

Consanguinity: The degree of relationship between persons who descend from a common ancestor. A father and son are related by lineal consanguinity, uncle and nephew by collateral sanguinity.

Consort: Wife, husband, spouse, mate, companion.

Consumption: Tuberculosis.

Conveyance: Legal document by which the title to property is transferred; warrant; patent; deed.

Cottar: A small holder.

Cousin: Child of an aunt or uncle; in earlier times a kinsman, close relative, or friend.

Creole: A person of European descent born in the West Indies or Spanish America. A person descended from or culturally related to the original French settlers of the southern United States, especially Louisiana. A Creolized language.

CW: Civil War, War of the Rebellion, War Between the States, 1861–1865.

D

d. (abbreviation): Died.

dau. (abbreviation): Daughter.

Daughter-in-law: A daughter-in-law is the wife of an individual's son. Daughter-in-law also used to mean "step-daughter."

Daughters of the American Revolution (DAR): Lineage organization for female descendants of Revolutionary War Soldiers, and others who aided in achieving American independence (1775-1783). The DAR is active in genealogical research and can be a source for those searching their family history if that history date back to the time of the revolutionary war.

Death Certificate: Documentation of Ones' death.

dec'd (abbreviation): Deceased.

Deceased: Commonly written "the deceased," meaning someone who has died.

Decedent: A deceased person.

Declaration of Intention: A declaration of intention is a document filed in a court by an alien who intended to become a United States citizen. It could also be a declaration filed by a couple in a local court, indicating their intention to marry.

Deed: Document transferring ownership and title of property.

Deposition: A testifying or testimony taken down in writing under oath of affirmation in reply to interrogatories, before a competent officer to replace to oral testimony of a witness.

Descendant: Children, grandchildren, great-grandchildren, and so on, anyone to whom you are an ancestor.

Descendant Chart: Report or chart that shows a person and all of their descendants in a graphical format - As opposed to the Modified register which is more of a narrative report.

Descent groups: A social group whose members claim common ancestry. A unilineal society (such as the Iroquois system) is one in which the descent of an individual is reckoned either from the mother's or the father's descent group. With matrilineal descent individuals belong to their mother's descent group (Not however through the mother directly. Usually descent is counted through the mother's brother, along with inheritance). With patrilineal descent, individuals belong to their father's descent group.

Devise: Gift of real property by last will and testament of the donor.

Devisee: Person receiving land or real property in the last will and testament of the donor.

Devisor: Person giving land or real property in a last will and testament.

Direct line: Line of decent traced through persons who are related to one another as a child and parent.

Directories: Directories come in all types: city, telephone, county, regional, professional, religious, post office, street, ethnic, and school. The directories you search will depend on the type of information you know about the individual. The information that you can find in a directory depends on the type of directory. For instance, a church directory may tell you about an individual's involvement in church activities, professional directories may give you insight into your ancestor's professional life, and club directories may contain information about your ancestor's involvement in social activities.

Dissenter: Name given a person who refused to belong to the established Church of England.

District land Office Plat Book: Books or rather maps which show the location of the land patentee.

District land office Tract Book: Books which list individual entries by range and township.

div. (abbreviation): Divorced.

DNA (Deoxyribonucleic Acid): The molecules inside cells that carry genetic information and pass it from one generation to the next. DNA is now used as a means of tracing genetic ancestry, and racial identity for Y (Male), and Mitochondria DNA.

Doomsday: Doomsday is a highly detailed survey and valuation of all the land held by the King and his chief tenants, along with all the resources that went with the land in late 11th century England.

Double Dating: The practice of writing double dates resulted from switching from the Julian to the Gregorian calendar, and also from the fact that not all countries and people accepted the new calendar at the same time.

Dowager: Widow holding property or a title received from her deceased husband; title given in England to widows of Princes, Dukes, Earls, and other Noblemen.

Dower: Legal provision of real estate and support made to the widow for her lifetime from a husband's estate.

Download: Downloading is electronically extracting files from a network or bulletin board system for use on your own computer. Many bulletin board systems with genealogy sections have files that you can download.

Dowry [also dowry]: Land, money, goods, or personal property brought by a bride to her husband in marriage.

Dropsy: Edema (swelling), often caused by kidney or heart disease.

Dropsy of the Brain: Encephalitis.

Dysentery: Inflammation of colon with frequent passage of mucous and blood.

E

Ecclesiastical Law: Biblical and Church law, stated as coming from God "ecclesiastic history".

Egypt: A country in North East Africa

Egyptian Hieroglyphs: One of the oldest writing systems in the world. Egyptian Hieroglyphs have been dated to between 3300 BC and 3200 BC (before Christ), using carbon isotopes. Pre-date the Sumerians of Mesopotamia, (Modern day Iraq).

Egyptian: Belonging or relating to Egypt, a country in NE Africa, its inhabitants, or their language. The earliest writing ever seen may have been discovered in southern Egypt. The hieroglyphics record linen and oil deliveries made over 5,000 years ago.

Elephantiasis: A form of leprosy

Emancipated: Freed from slavery; freed from parents' control; of legal age.

Emigrant: Person leaving one country to reside in another country.

Emigrate: When an individual from one region moves into another country or region.

Encephalitis: Swelling of brain; aka sleeping sickness.

Enfeoff: To grant property in fee simple; as in a deed the seller "does grant, bargain, sell, alien, enfeoff, release, and confirm unto the buyer" certain property.

English Common Law: In. the traditional unwritten law of England, based on custom and usage, which began to develop over a thousand years before the founding of the United States. The best of the pre-Saxon compendiums of the common law was reportedly written by a woman, Queen Martia, wife of a king of a small English kingdom.

Entail: To entail is to restrict the inheritance of land to a specific group of heirs, such as an individual's sons.

Enteric fever: Typhoid fever.

Enumeration: List of people, as in a census.

Epitaph: An inscription on or at a tomb or grave in memory of the one buried there.

Escheat: The reversion of property to the state when there are no qualified heirs.

Estate: Assets and liabilities of a decedent, including land, personal belongings and debts.

et al: And others.

et ux: And wife.

et uxor: And his wife. Sometimes written simply et ux.

Ethnic: A community, or group of people sharing a common and distinctive racial, national, religious, linguistic, or cultural heritage. Members of a particular ethnic group, especially belonging to a national group by heritage or culture but residing outside its national boundaries, eg., Africans living in America.

Eugenics: The selection of desired heritable characteristics in order to improve future generations, typically in reference to humans. The term eugenics was coined in 1883 by the British explorer and natural scientist Francis Galton, who advocated a system that would allow "the more suitable races or strains of blood."

Evidence: Any kind of proof, such as testimony, documents, records, certificates, material objects, etc.

exec. (abbreviation): Executor.

Executor: Male appointed by a testator to carry out the directions and requests in his or her will, and to dispose of the property according to his testamentary provisions after his or her death.

Executrix: Female appointed by a testator to carry out the directions and requests in his or her will, and to dispose of the property according to the testamentary provisions after his or her death.

exor. (abbreviation): Executor.

exox. (abbreviation): Executrix.

F

Falling sickness: Epilepsy.

fam. (abbreviation): Family.

Family group sheet: A family group sheet is a form which presents genealogical information about a nuclear family—a husband, a wife, and their children. A family group sheet usually includes birth dates and places, death dates and places, and marriage dates and places. Family Tree Maker for Windows can help you create family group sheets for your family.

Family histories/genealogies: Family histories and genealogies are books which detail the basic genealogical facts about one or more generations of a particular family.

Family History Center (FHC): A smaller branch of the FHL, found nationwide.

Family History Library (FHL): Located in Salt Lake City, Utah. Houses an extensive collection of written manuscripts including family histories, local histories, indexes, periodicals, and aids to help in genealogical research.

Family pedigrees: In general, family pedigrees refer to family group sheets that are linked in a computer system. When you access an individual's family group sheet in a linked pedigree, you also access all of the records that are linked to that individual.

Father-in-Law: Father of one's spouse.

Fee: An estate of inheritance in land, being either fee simple or fee tail. An estate in land held of a feudal lord on condition of the performing of certain services.

Fee simple: Absolute ownership of land to sell or devise without restriction.

Fee Tail: An estate of inheritance limited to lineal descendant heirs of a person to whom it was granted.

Feme: Female, woman, or wife.

Feme sole: Unmarried woman or a married woman with property independent of her husband.

Feudal: Term given much later to the medieval system of land tenure in which the King or a baron gave land and protection to his tenants in return for their loyalty and specific services, principally military.

Fits: Sudden attack or seizure of muscle activity.

Five Civilized Tribes: Five Indian tribes or nations, Cherokees, Chickasaws, Choctaws, Creeks, and Seminoles; that lived in the Southeastern United States; until the removal act of 1830 was passed. They were removed to Oklahoma Territory from 1830-42. Most of the tribes had set up formal governments before removal modeled after the US government. The Freed slaves (called Freedmen), were also removed to Oklahoma.

Flux: An excessive flow or discharge of fluid like hemorrhage or diarrhea.

Fortnight: Two weeks.

FPC (Free People of Color): A Pre-Civil War term used to identify, persons of color, Blacks, Natives, Mulattoes, who were free.

FPOC (Free Person of Color): A term used to denote persons of color who were born free and/or manumitted. The term encompassed Free Blacks, Natives, and persons of mixed raced heritage, in Colonial America.

FR (abbreviation): Family register.

Franklin, State Of: An area once known but never officially recognized and was under consideration from 1784 – 1788 from the western part of North Carolina.

Fraternity: Group of men (or women) sharing a common purpose or interest.

Free Hold: An estate in fee simple, in fee tail, or for life.

Free Person of Color: See FPOC

Freedman: Male released from slavery; emancipated person.

Freehold: An estate in fee simple, in fee tail, or for life.

French pox: Syphilis

Friend: Member of the Religious Society of Friends; a Quaker.

Full age: Age of majority; legal age; adult (legal age varied according to place and current law).

Furlong: 1,000 links; 660 feet.

G

Gazetteer: A book which alphabetically names and describes the places in a specific area. For example, a gazetteer of a county would name and describe all of the towns, lakes, rivers, and mountains in the county.

gdn.: Guardian.

GEDCOM Database: Genealogy Data Communications, a standardized format for genealogy databases that allows the exchange of data among different software programs and operating systems.

Genealogy: Genealogy is the study of ancestry or family lineage. The genealogist usually records lines of descent by a pedigree chart or family tree. Genealogy is as old as recorded history, e.g. the Bible chronicles family lineage in both the Old and New Testaments, and royalty lines are noted in the annals of the ancient Sumerian, Babylonian, etc. empires.

Genetic Genealogy: A means of tracing ancestry through DNA.

Gentleman: A man well born.

Ghana: The Republic of Ghana is a country in West Africa. It borders Côte d'Ivoire to the west, Burkina Faso to the north, Togo to the east, and the Gulf of Guinea to the south. It was the first sub-Saharan country to obtain independence from colonial rule.

Given Name: Name given to a person at birth or baptism, one's first and middle names (in societies where the surname is inherited).

Glebe: Land belonging to a parish church.

Good brother: brother-in-law.

Good sister: Sister-in-law.

Good son: Son-in-law.

Granddame: Grandmother.

Grantee: One who buys property or receives a grant.

Grantee index: Master index of persons purchasing, buying or receiving property.

Grantor: One who sells property or makes a grant.

Grantor index: Master index of persons selling, granting, transferring or conveying property.

grdn. (abbreviation): Guardian.

Great pox: Syphilis.

Great-Aunt: Sister of one's grandparent (also grand-aunt).

Great-Uncle: Brother of one's grandparent (also grand-uncle).

Grippe/grip: Influenza like symptoms.

Gullah: *A unique culture that is directly linked to West Africa. In South Carolina, this group of African-Americans and the language they speak are referred to as Gullah (Gul-luh). In Georgia, they are called Geechee (Gee-chee). Native Islanders is another term that refers to the Gullah and Geechee people.*

Guardian: Person lawfully appointed to care for the person of a minor, invalid, incompetent and their interests, such as education, property management and investments.

H

Half Brother/Half Sister: The relationship of siblings who have only one parent in common.

Head Right: Rights to a certain number of acres (usually 50) of land guaranteed in advance for each settler in a new territory. Virginia was settled by this method in the 17th century.

Head Tax: Tax on people, also called a poll tax or capitation.

Heat stroke: Body temperature elevates because of surrounding environment temperature and body does not perspire to reduce temperature. Coma and death result if not reversed.

Heir: Person who succeeds, by the rules of law, to an estate upon the death of an ancestor; one with rights to inherit an estate.

Heir apparent: By law a person, whose right of inheritance is established, provided he or she outlives the ancestor, see also primogeniture.

Heir: Those entitled by law or by the terms of a will to inherit property from another.

Holographic Will: A holographic or olographic will is handwritten and signed by the individual that the will belongs to.

Homestead: A homestead usually is a home on land obtained from the United States government. Part of the agreement between the individual and the government was that the individual had to live on the land and make improvements to it, such as adding buildings and clearing fields.

Homestead Act: Law passed by Congress in 1862 allowing a head of a family to obtain title to 160 acres of public land after clearing and improving it for 5 years.

hon. (abbreviation): Honorable.

Householder: In England, a householder is one who inhabits a dwelling or tenement of such a nature as to qualify him for the exercise of the franchise. The word "house-keeper" was formerly synonymous with "householder."

Housekeeper: In England, a *householder* is one who inhabits a dwelling or tenement of such a nature as to qualify him for the exercise of the franchise. The word "house-keeper" was formerly synonymous with "householder.

Huguenot: French Protestants who fled from religious persecution.

Hundred: A military and administrative district, dating to the 10th C. under King Ethelred, but in use as late as the 17th C., in early British colonial America. A hundred is not 100 acres but 100 hides, one of which will support a family of that day. Each hide varied from 60 to 120 acres depending on the quality of

---

the land. Famous American hundreds were Bermuda Hundred, and Martin's Hundred which had at least 21,500 acres in the first settlement and 200 settlers.

husb. (abbreviation): husband.

I

Illegitimate: Child born to unmarried parents.

Immigrant: Person moving into a country from another country.

Immigration: When an individual goes into a new country to live.

imp. (abbreviation): Imported.

In solemn will: Will in which an executor is not appointed.

Indenture: Today it means a contract in two or more copies. Originally made in two parts by cutting or tearing a single sheet across the middle in a jagged line so the two parts may later be matched.

Indentured servant: Person who bound into the service of another person for a specified period, usually seven years in the 18th and 19th centuries to pay for passage to another country. At one point in Colonial Virginia, persons identified as Mulatto were by law to serve Indentures (thirty years for females – twenty years for males).

Index: In genealogical terms, an alphabetical list of names taken from a particular set of records. For example, a census record index lists the names of individuals that are found in a particular set of census records. Indexes usually come in book form, but you can also find them on CD-ROM, microfilm, and microfiche.

Indian: (Also see Native American) According to the Bureau of Indian Affairs, no single Federal or tribal criterion establishes a person's identity as an Indian. Government agencies use differing criteria to determine who is an Indian eligible to participate in their programs. Tribes also have varying eligibility criteria for membership. To determine what the criteria might be for agencies or Tribes, one must contact them directly.

Inf.: Infantry.

Infant: Young Child.

Infantile paralysis: Polio.

Inst. (abbreviation): Instant.

Instant: Of or pertaining to the current month. (Abbreviated inst.).

Intentions: Public notification of an upcoming marriage, (see banns).

International Genealogical Index (IGI): One of the resources of the Family History Library of the Church of Jesus Christ of Latter-day Saints. Containing approximately 250 million names, it is an index of people's names that were either submitted to the church, or were extracted from records that the church has microfilmed over the years. You can use the IGI to locate information about your ancestors.

Intestate: Denote a person who died without leaving a will.

Intestinal colic: Abdominal pain due to improper diet

Inventory: A legal list of all the property in a deceased person's estate. The executor of the will is required to make an inventory.

Issue: Derogatory term used to describe children, descendants, and offspring of Native Americans in Virginia, coined by Walter Plecker

J

Jail fever: Typhus

Jaundice: Condition caused by blockage of intestines

jno (abbreviation): John or Johannes.

Joiner: Carpenter who does finish work.

jud. (abbreviation): Judicial.

Julian Calendar: Calendar named for Julius Caesar and used from 45 B.C. to 1582, called the "Old Style" calendar; replaced by the Gregorian calendar.

junr. (abbreviation): Junior.

Juvenis: Juvenile, minor, under legal age.

K

Kinship: The most basic principle of organizing individuals into social groups, roles, and categories.

Kinship and descent: One of the major concepts of cultural anthropology. Cultures worldwide possess a wide range of systems of tracking kinship and descent. Anthropologists break these down into simple concepts which are common among many different cultures.

Knave: Servant boy.

L

Land Patent: The document which states the settler had a permanent

Land records: Land records are deeds—proof that a piece of land is owned by a particular individual. The information you receive from the records will vary, but you will at least get a name, the location of the property, and the period of ownership.

Land Right: The legal obligations which are attached to ownership of land

Land Warrant: A certificate issued by a land office which entitled the holder to land.

Late: Denoting someone who is deceased, ie., the late John Thomas.

Lease: An agreement which creates a landlord - tenant situation.

Legacy: Property or money bequeathed to someone in a will.

Legatee: Someone who inherits money or property from a person who left a will.

Legislature: Lawmaking branch of state or national government; elected group of lawmakers.

Lessee: Person leasing property from an owner.

Lesser: Owner leasing property to a tenant.

Letters Testamentary: Court document allowing the executor named in a will to carry out his or her duties.

Liber: Book of public records.

lic. (abbreviation): License.

Lien: Claim placed on property by a person who is owed money.

Life estate: Use interest in property until death.

Lineage: Direct line of descent from common ancestor; ancestry; progeny.

Lineal: Consisting of or being in a direct line of ancestry or descendants; descended in a direct line.

Link: Length 1/100th of a surveying chain; 7.92 inches

Lis pendens: Notices of lawsuit, and pending litigation, usually in matters concerning land.

Litigant: Person involved in a lawsuit.

liv. (abbreviation): Living.

Local history: A local history is usually a book about a particular town or county. Local histories were quite popular in the late 19th century. While they often give the history of the development of the area, they usually also include some information about the important families that lived there.

Lockjaw: Tetanus or infectious disease affecting the muscles of the neck and jaw. Untreated, it is fatal in eight days.

Loco Parentis: In place of the parent or parents.

Lodge: A chapter or meeting hall of a fraternal organization.

Long sickness: Tuberculosis.

Loyalist: Colonist who supported the British during the American Revolution; Tory.

ltd. (abbreviation): Limited.

M

m. (abbreviation): Married.

Maiden name: A woman's last name prior to marriage.

Major: Person who has reached legal age.

Majores: Ancestors.

Majority: Legal age.

Mali Empire: An Islamic Empire of the Mandinka people in West Africa from the 14th through 17th centuries. The empire was ruled by Mansa (King), Sundiata Keita. He was known for his generosity and wealth, and for the fabled wealth of the city of Timbuktu.

Mali: A landlocked republic in northwestern Africa; achieved independence from France in 1960; Mali was a center of West African civilization for more than 4,000 years. A land-locked nation in West Africa, and the second largest country among West African nations. It borders Algeria on the north, Niger on the east, Burkina Faso and the Ivory Coast on the south, Guinea on the south-west, and Senegal and Mauritania on the west.

Manse: Parsonage; enough land to support a family.

Manumission: Manumission is the act of being released from slavery or servitude.

Manuscript: Manuscripts are usually unpublished family histories or collections of family papers. Depending on what the manuscript contains, you may be able to find all kinds of family information. Generally, you will find more than just names, birth dates, and death dates.

Marita: Married woman, wife.

Maritus: Bridegroom, married man.

Marriage Bond: A marriage bond is document obtained by an engaged couple prior to their marriage. It affirmed that there was no moral or legal reason why the couple could not be married. In addition, the man affirmed that he would be able to support himself and his new bride.

Marriage contract: A legal agreement between prospective spouses made before marriage to determine their property rights and those of their children.

Marriage records: A marriage record contains information about a marriage between two individuals. On a marriage record, you can at least find the bride's and grooms full names, the date of the marriage, and county where the marriage took place. Many marriage records include other information, such as the names and birthplaces of the bride's and groom's parents, the addresses of the bride and groom, information about previous marriages, and the names of the witnesses to the marriage.

Maternal line: A line of descent traced through the mother's ancestry.

Maternal: Related through one's mother, such as a Maternal grandmother being the mother's mother.

Matrilineage: Line of descent as traced through women on the maternal side of a family.

Matron: An older married woman with children.

md. (abbreviation): Married.

Measurements: Link - 7.92 inches; Chain - 100 Links or 66 feet; Furlong - 1000 Links or 660 feet; Rod - 5 ½ yds or 16 ½ ft (also called a perch or pole); Rod - From 5 ½ yards to 8 yards, depending on locality; Acre - 43,560 square ft or 160 square rods

Melungeons: Mixed raced people of Native, black, white descent, living in the Mountains of Tennessee

Mensis: Month.

Messuage: A dwelling house.

Mestizo: A person of mixed blood; a person of mixed Spanish and Amer-indian blood.

Metes: Measurements of distance in feet, rods, poles, chains, etc.; pertains to measuring direction and distance.

Metes and bounds: Method of surveying property by using physical and topographical features in conjunction with measurements.

Microfiche: Sheet of microfilm with greatly reduced images of pages of documents.

Microfilm: Reproduction of documents on film at reduced size.

Migrant: Person who moves from place to place, usually in search of work.

Migrate: To move from one country or state or region to another.

Migration: The move from one area to another.

mil. (abbreviation): Military.

Military Certificate: a document stating that a person's proof of military service had been presented to the proper authorities and, therefore, he was eligible for a specific amount of land as compensation. There was only one claim to this type of land available to each person.

Military Land: Public land which was reserved for Revolutionary or War of 1812 soldiers to receive as part of their compensation for service.

Military Records: Records kept by the United States Government on Military and Civilian Personnel. Most files have very detailed information, such as the individual's name, their spouse's name, date of birth, place of residence, which wars the individual served in; which branch of the service, (Navy, Marines, or Army); when the individual's service began and ended, where and when the individual died, and where the individual was buried.

Military Warrant: A document issued by the land office requesting that land be set aside for a veteran entitled to it for his military service. The land was located in Ohio and Kentucky and eligibility for its ownership was based upon the veteran's military certificate.

Militia: A citizen army; a military organization formed by local citizens to serve in emergencies.

Minner: Person who surrenders land to another in exchange for release from contractual obligations.

Minor: A person under legal age; historically, the legal age differed from place to place and over time. (Check prevailing law to determine the legal age requirement at a specific time.)

Mister: In early times, a title of respect given only to those who held important Civil Officer, or who were of gentle blood.

Mitochondrial DNA. (mtDNA): A type of DNA that is carried by both men and women but is only inherited from the mother. Mothers in turn, inherit their DNA from their mothers ... and so on back in time along one's maternal line. Human mtDNA is a powerful tool for tracking matrilineal lines, and has been used in this role for tracking the ancestry of many species back hundreds of generations.

mo. (abbreviation): Month.

Moiety: A indefinite portion.

Moor: A member of a Muslim people of mixed Berber and Arab descent, now living chiefly in northwest Africa. A group of Muslims who invaded Spain in the 8th century and established a civilization in Andalusia that lasted until the late 15th century.

Mortality: Death; death rate.

Mortality Schedule: Enumeration of persons who died during the year prior to June 1 of 1850, 1860, 1870, and 1880 in each state of the United States, conducted by the bureau of census.

Mortgage: A conditional transfer of title to real property as security for payment of a debt.

Mother-in-Law: Mother of one's spouse.

Mulatto: A mixed raced person of white/African and/or Native heritage.

Mustee: Mixed raced Native & Spanish (also see Mestizo).

N

n.d. (abbreviation): No date; not dated.

n.p. (abbreviation): No place listed; no publisher listed.

na.: Naturalized; not applicable.

Namesake: The person after whom an individual is named

Native American: The indigenous peoples from the regions of North and South America, which now including the continental United States, including parts of Alaska. They comprise a large number of distinct tribes, states, and ethnic groups, many of which are still enduring as political communities

Naturalization records: Naturalization records document the process by which an immigrant becomes a citizen. An individual has to live in the United States for a specific period of time and file a series of forms with a court before he or she can become naturalized. Naturalization records provide the following information: place and date of birth, date of arrival into the United States, place of residence at the time of naturalization, a personal description, and sometimes the name of the ship that the individual arrived on and the individual's occupation.

Natus: Born.

Necrology: Listing or record of persons who have died recently.

Nee: Born, used to denote a woman's maiden name, i.e., Anne Gibson nee West.

Negro: Often Offensive. References to persons of African descent. Not a scientific term.

neph. (abbreviation): Nephew.

Nephew: Son of one's brother or sister.

Newspaper announcements: Normally, newspapers announce events of genealogical interest such as births, deaths, and marriages. The amount of information in these announcements will vary. Most likely you will find the names of the individuals involved in the event, the date of the event, and where the event took place. Sometimes you can even find pictures.

Niece: Daughter of one's brother or sister.

Noncupative Will: One declared or dictated by the testator, usually for persons in last sickness, sudden illness, or military.

Nuclear family: Western model of Nuclear family is two parents and children. The nuclear family is ego-centered and impermanent, while descent groups are permanent (lasting beyond the lifespans of individual constituents) and reckoned according to a single ancestor.

nunc. (abbreviation): nuncupative will, oral will.

O

ob. (abbreviation): Obit, deceased,

obiit. (abbreviation): He or she died.

obit. (abbreviation): Obituary.

Obituary: A notice of someone's death; usually includes a short biography

Octaroon: Child of a quadroon; person having one-eighth black ancestry.

Of color: A Colonial term used to denote persons other than Europeans eg., black, Indian, and persons of mixed blood.

Old Dominion: Virginia: a state in the eastern United States; one of the original 13 colonies; one of the Confederate States in the American Civil War.

Old style calendar: Julian calendar, used before the Gregorian calendar.

Olographic Will: See Holographic Will.

Oral history: An oral history is a collection of family stories told by a member of the family or by a close family friend. Normally, an oral history is transcribed onto paper, or is video or tape recorded. Oral histories can yield some of the best information about a family—the kinds of things that you won't find written in records.

Oral will: Nuncupative will - oral will declare or dictated by the testator in his last sickness before a sufficient number of witnesses and afterwards put in writing.

Orphan asylum: An orphanage.

Orphan: A child whose mother, father, or both have died.

Orphan's Court: Orphans being recognized as wards of the states provisions were made for them in special courts.

OS: Old style calendar.

Overseer: A person in charge of work on a plantation. People who lived along it and used the road most frequently. Purchased the materials to be used in work done by the unemployed.

Overseer of the Poor: In Colonial days the person appointed to this post. He also dispensed aid to the poor.

Overseer of the Road: A person appointed to maintain a specified stretch of road. He obtained workers to care for the road from the

P

p.o.a. (abbreviation): Power of attorney.

p.r. (abbreviation): Parish registers.

Palatinate: Area in Germany known as the Pfalz, Rhineland Pfalz, and Bavarian Pfalz, from which thousands of families immigrated to colonial America.

Paleography: Study of handwriting.

Parent County: The County from which a new county is formed.

Parish: Ecclesiastical division or jurisdiction; the site of a church. Also a county in Louisiana.

Passenger Lists: Passenger lists are lists of the names and information about passengers that arrived on ships into the United States. These lists were submitted to customs collectors at every port by the ship's master. Passenger lists were not officially required by the United States government until 1820. Before that date, the information about each passenger varied widely, from names to number of bags.

Patent: A government grant of property in fee simple to public lands; land grant.

Paternal: Belonging to or inherited from one's father; "spent his childhood on the paternal farm"; "paternal traits

Paternity: The state of being a father.

Patrilineal: Relating to, based on, or tracing ancestral descent through the paternal line.

Patriot: One who loves his country and supports its interests.

Patronymics: Patronymics is the practice of creating last names from the name of one's father. For example, Robert, John's son, would become Robert Johnson. Robert Johnson's son Neil would become Neil Robertson.

Pedigree: Family tree; ancestry.

Pedigree chart: A chart showing a person's ancestry.

Pension (military): A benefit paid regularly to a person for military service or a military service related disability.

Pensioner: A person who receives pension benefits.

Perch: 5 ½ yards; a pole; a rod.

Pole: See measurements.

Poll: Used in early tax records denoting a taxable person; person eligible to vote.

Post: Latin prefix meaning after, as in post-war economy.

Posterity: Descendants; those who come after.

Posthumous: A child born after the death of the father.

Power of Attorney: A written instrument whereon persons, as principal, appoints someone as his or her agent, thereby authorizing that person to perform certain acts on behalf of the principal, such as buying or selling property, settling an estate, representing them in court, etc.

pr. (abbreviation): Proved, probated.

Pre: Latin prefix meaning before, as in pre-war build-up.

Pre-Emotion Rights: Right given by the federal government to citizens, to buy a quarter section of land or less.

Preponderance of evidence: Evidence of greater weight or more convincing than the opposing evidence; evidence more credible and convincing, more reasonable and probable, and can be circumstantial in nature.

Primary evidence: Original or first-hand evidence; the best evidence available that must be used before secondary evidence can be introduced as proof.

Primary source: Primary sources are records that were created at the time of an event. For example, a primary source for a birth date would be a birth certificate. While you can find birth dates on other documents, such as marriage certificates, they would not be primary sources for the birth date, because they were not created at the time of the birth.

Primogeniture: Insures the right of the eldest son to inherit the entire estate of his parents, to the exclusion of younger sons.

prob. (abbreviation): Probably; probated.

Probate: Legal process used to determine the validity of a will before the court authorizes distribution of an estate; legal process used to appoint someone to administer the estate of someone who died without leaving a will.

Probate records: Probate records are records disposing of a deceased individual's property. They may include an individual's last will and testament, if one was made. The information you can get from probate records varies, but usually includes the name of the deceased, either the deceased's age at the time of death or birth date, property, members of the family, and the last place of residence.

Progenitor: A direct ancestor.

Progeny: Descendants of a common ancestor; issue.

Proved Will: A will established as genuine by probate court.

Provost: A person appointed to superintend, or preside over something.

Proximo: In the following month, in the month after the present one.

Public domain: Land owned by a government.

Pvt. (abbreviation): Military rank of private

Q

Quaker: Member of the Religious Society of Friends.

Quadroon: The child of a mulatto and white parentage; a child with one black grandparent.

Quitclaim: A deed conveying the interest of the party at that time.

Quitclaim deed: Transfer of land or claim without guaranteeing a clear title.

Quit rent roll: In early Virginia, a list of those who paid the annual fee to the King in exchange for the right to live on and farm property.

R

R.C.: (abbreviation): Roman Catholic.

Race: A local geographic or global human population distinguished as a more or less distinct group by physical characteristics. Humans considered as a group. There are three racial classifications, African, Asiatic, and Caucasian.

Racial: Of, relating to, or characteristic of race or races. Arising from or based on differences among human racial groups.

Real Property: Land and anything attached to it, such as houses, building, barns, growing timber, growing crops, etc.

Rec'd (abbreviation): Received.

Receiver: Person appointed by court to hold property until a suit is settled.

Reconveyance: The transferring of a title back to its previous owner.

Rector: A clergyman; the ruler or governor of a country.

Reeve: Churchwarden; early name for sheriff in England.

reg. (abbreviation): Register.

Relict: Widow; surviving spouse when one has died, husband or wife.

Relicta: Widow.

Relictus: Widower.

Repository: The place where a source can be found (i.e., Library, FHC, etc.).

Republic: Government in which supreme authority lies with the people or their elected representatives.

repud. (abbreviation): Repudiate.

res. (abbreviation: Residence; research.

Researcher ID card: All researchers using original records at the National Archives or National Archives regional centers must get a researcher ID card. If you just plan to use microfilmed records, you do not need to get an ID card. To get an ID card you will be asked to fill out an application. You should bring photo identification, such as a driver's license, school identification card, or passport on your first visit to the archives. Researcher ID cards are free of charge and are valid for two years. The ID card must be presented at each visit.

Reservation: To Reserve, to set aside. In the United States, these reserves are lands set aside for the exclusive use of Native Americans. After independence, the United States adopted a national policy of Indian administration by Constitutional mandate. After 1778, Congress established federal Indian reservations by federal treaty or statute, conferring to the occupying tribe(s) recognized title over lands and the resources within their boundaries. The Constitution granted Congress plenary powers over Indian affairs in trade, treaties, warfare, welfare, and the right to take Indian lands for public purposes. Despite government promises of protection in exchange for land cessions, Secretary of War Henry Knox in 1789 lamented, "that all the Indian tribes once existing in those States, now the best cultivated and most populous, have become extinct

ret. (abbreviation): Retired.

Rev. (abbreviation): Reverend.

Rev. War (abbreviation): Revolutionary War.

Revolutionary War: The war between the American colonies and Great Britain (1775–1783), leading to the formation of the independent United States.

Rod: See measurements.

Rood: 5 ½ to 8 yards depending upon location; ¼ of an acre.

Rustica: Country girl.

Rusticus: Country boy.

S

s. & h. (abbreviation): Son and heir.

s. (abbreviation): Son.

s/o: Son of.

Secondary evidence: Evidence that is inferior to primary evidence or the best evidence.

Secondary source: A secondary source is a record that was created a significant amount of time after an event occurred. For example, a marriage certificate would be a secondary source for a birth date, because the birth took place several years before the time of the marriage. However, that same marriage certificate would be a primary source for a marriage date, because it was created at the time of the marriage.

Self Addressed Stamped Envelope (SASE): When you request records or other information from people and institutions, you should include a self-addressed stamped envelope (SASE) in your letter. If you are expecting return mail from overseas, you should include an International Reply Coupon with your self-addressed envelope. This coupon serves as payment for any international postage you may need to pay. They can be purchased at your local post office.

serv. (abbreviation): Servant.

Shaker: Member of a religious group formed in 1747 which practiced communal living and celibacy.

Sibling: A brother or sister, persons who share the same parents in common.

Sic: A Latin term signifying a copy reads exactly as the original; indicates a possible mistake in the original.

soc. (abbreviation): Society

Social security death index: An index of Social Security Death records. Generally this includes names of deceased Social Security recipients whose relatives applied for Social Security Death Benefits after their passing. Also included in the millions of records are approximately 400,000 railroad retirement records from the early 1900s to 1950s.

Son-in-law: Husband of one's daughter.

Soundex: Phonetic indexing system.

Source: A book, document, record, publication, manuscript, etc. used to prove a fact.

Spinster: Unmarried woman; woman acting in her own right.

Sponsor: A sponsor is an individual other than the parents of a child that takes responsibility for the child's religious education. Sponsors are usually present at a child's baptism. Sponsors are often referred to as godparents.

Spouse: Husband or wife.

srnm. (abbreviation): Surname, last name.

St. (abbreviation): Saint; street.

Statute: A law.

Step: Used in conjunction with a degree of kinship.

Step-Brother/Step-Sister: Child of one's step-father or step-mother.

Stepchild: Child of one of the spouses by a former marriage who has not been adopted by the step-parent.

Stepfather: Husband of a child's mother by a later marriage.

Stepmother: Wife of a child's father by a later marriage.

Succession: Legal term in the transfer of property to legal heirs of an intestate estate. Probate; process of determining a will's validity identifying heirs, etc.

Sundiata Keita: The founder of the Mali Empire in West Africa, (b. ca. 1210- d. ca. 1260). He is now regarded as a great magician-king and the national hero of the Malinke-speaking people.

surg. (abbreviation): Surgeon

Surname: Last name, family name.

T

T. (abbreviation): Township.

terr. (abbreviation): Territory.

Territory: Area of land owned b the United States, not a state, but having its own legislature.

test. (abbreviation): Testament.

Testamentary: Pertaining to a will.

Testate: Died leaving a valid will.

Testator: Man who writes a valid will.

Testatrix: Woman who writes a valid will.

Testis: Witness.

Tippling House. A place where spirituous liquors are sold and drunk in violation of law. Sometimes the mere selling is considered as evidence of keeping a tippling house.

Tithable: A person taxable by law.

Tithe: In English law, the tenth part of one's annual increase paid to support noblemen and clergy; amount of annual poll tax.

Tory: Loyalist; one who supported the British side in the American Revolution.

Township: In a government survey, is a square tract six miles on each side containing thirty-six square miles of land; a name given to the civil and political subdivisions of a county.

Tradition: The handing down of statements, beliefs, legends, customs, genealogies, etc., from generation to generation; especially by word of mouth.

Trail of Tears: The Trail of Tears refers to the forced relocation in 1838 of the Cherokee Native American tribe to the Western United States. In the Cherokee language, the event is called Nunna daul Isunyi—"The Trail Where We Cried." Also on the Trail of Tears were slaves, owned by the Cherokee, (now known as Freedmen).

Transcribe: To make a copy in writing.

Tri Racial: Historically persons of mixed Native/White/African ancestry.

Tri Racial Isolates: Persons of mixed Native/White/African ancestry, usually living in isolated or rural areas (Mountains of Tennessee, Blue Ridge Mountains Virginia, Welsh Mountain area in Eastern Pennsylvania). The racial identity given to these individuals is usually black or white.

Tsalagi: (Real People) Iroquoian language with an innovative written syllabi invented by a Cherokee scholar. Most of the Native Literature published today, is published in the Tsalagi Language. It is still an imperiled language because of government policies as late as the fifties which enforced the removal of Cherokee children from The Tsalagi Language speaking homes, reducing the number of young Cherokees being raised bilingually.

Tutor: (in Louisiana) A guardian of minor children.

Tutrix: Feminine form of tutor.

twp.: (abbreviation): Township.

U

Ultimo: The preceding month

Underground Railroad: Neither Underground, nor a railroad, but a network of people that helped slaves escape to the north and Canada. On the Underground Railroad, blacks and whites assisted fugitive slaves. Between 1810 and 1850 this was one of the most effective ways for a slave to escape.

Union: The United States; also the North during the Civil War, the states which did not secede.

unk. (abbreviation): Unknown

Unprobated will: Will not submit for probate.

unm. (abbreviation): Unmarried.

United States Colored Troops (USCT): Units of Black and mixed raced soldiers, who fought in the Civil War.

uxor.: Wife, spouse, consort.

V

Valid: That which is legal and binding.

Verbatim: Word for word; in the same words, verbally.

Vendue: Public Auction.

Vestry: Administrative group within a parish; the ruling body of a church.

Vidua: Widow.

Viduus: Widower.

Virgo: Used to describe an unmarried woman in English and European marriage records.

Vital records: Birth, marriage, and death records.

Vital Statistics: Data dealing with birth, death, marriage or divorce.

W

Wales: The name given to the federated Tribes of Ancient Britain. The peoples occupying the land referred to themselves poetically as "Gwails". The federated tribes of ancient Britain who together contested the soil of their native land with the Germanic invader. In Welsh Cymru means Wales, Cymro a Welshman, Cymracs a Welshwoman, and Cymry Welshmen.

War Between the States: U.S. Civil War, 1861 - 1865.

Ward: Chiefly the division of a city for election purposes.

Warranty deed: Guarantees a clear property title from the seller to the buyer.

Wheelwright: Person who makes and repairs vehicle wheels, such as carts, wagons, etc.

White rent: Blackmail; rent to be paid in silver.

Widow: A widow is a woman whose husband has died.

Widower: A widower is a man whose wife has died.

Will: A document stating how a person wants real and personal property divided after death.

Witness: A witness is an individual present at an event such as a marriage or the signing of a document and can vouch that the event took place.

WPA Historical Records Survey: A program undertaken by the US Government from 1935 - 1936, in which inventories were compiled of historical material.

Writ of attachment: Court order authorizing the seizure of property sufficient to cover debts and court costs for not appearing in court.

Writ of summons: Document ordering a person to appear in court.

Y

Y-Chromosome: Y-chromosome DNA (Y-DNA) is a type of DNA that is only carried by men and is only inherited from their fathers. Men who share a common paternal ancestor will have virtually the same Y-DNA, even if that male ancestor lived many generations ago.

Yeoman: Farmer; freeholder who works a small estate; rank below gentleman.

Selected Bibliography

≠ ≠

Acts of the Assembly. "An Act to Preserve Racial Integrity." Approved March 20, 1924.

Amherst County Marriage Records, 1855–1957. Amherst County Courthouse, Amherst Virginia

Berry, Brewton (1963). Almost White. New York: MacMillan Company.

Coffey, Reverend EVA. (1998). The Diocese of Virginia. Fifteen Existing Parish Registers of the Colonial Established Church of Virginia (Episcopal) and Their Location, Richmond Virginia

Cook, M. (1984). The Pioneer Lewis Families. Indiana: Cook Publications, Vol. IV

Curtis, Natalie (1907). The Indians Book. New York & London: Harper and Row Bros.

Dictionary of American History—Cherokee. New York. Charles Scribner and Sons.

Ehle, J. (1988). Trail of Tears—The Rise and fall of the Cherokee Nation. New York: Archer Books.

Fairmount Baptist Church (1969). Membership Roll

Forbes, J.D. (1988). Black Africans and Native Americans. "Native Americans as Mulattoes." New York: Basil Blackwell, Incorporated.

Franklin, J. H. (1980). From Slavery to Freedom: A History of Negro Americans, (Fifth Edition), New York: Alfred A. Knopf.

From Creole to African: Atlantic Creoles and the Origins of African-American Society in Mainland North America.

The William & Mary Quarterly, Third Series, LIII, p. 254 note 8.

Heinegg, P. (1993). Free African Americans of North Carolina and Virginia: including the history of more than 80% of those counted as "all other free persons" in the 1790 and 1800 census. Maryland: Genealogical Publishing Co.

Heingg, P. (1994). Free African-Americans of North Carolina and Virginia. Maryland: Heritage Press.

Hening, W. W. Statutes at Large [II: 280] Virginia: The Library of Virginia.

Hening, W.W. (1823). The Statutes at Large, Vol. IV. Philadelphia: Thomas DeSilver Publishing

Hodges, M. E. (1981). A Brief Relation of Virginia Pre-History. Virginia: Virginia Research Center for Archaeology.

Houck, P. W. & Markham, M. D. (1993). Indian Island. Virginia: Warwick House Publishing.

In Lauber, A.W. (1970). Indian Slavery in Colonial Times. Williamstown, Massachusetts.

Jacobsen, D. (1970). Great Indian Tribes. NY: Hammond Press Inc.

Jefferson, T. (1786). Notes on the State Of Virginia, London England.

Katz, W.L. (1997). Black Indians A Hidden Heritage. New York: Aladdin Paperbacks.

Kenner Family (1901). William & Mary Quarterly Historical Magazine, Vol. 9, No. 3. Virginia: Williamsburg

Lauber, A.W. (1970). Indian Slaves in Colonial Times within the Present Limits of the United States. Massachusetts: Corner House Publishers.

McElroy, S.S. & W. (1997). Passages—A History of Amherst County. Virginia: Peddler Press.

McElroy, W. & S. (1993). Strangers in Their Midst. Maryland: Heritage Books.

Mcllwaine, Executive Journals of the Council, [III: 332]. Virginia: The Library of Virginia

Percy, A. (1961). The Amherst County Story. Virginia: Percy Press.

Rice, H. (1995). The Buffalo Ridge Cherokees: Remnants of a Great Nation Divided. Maryland: Heritage Books.

Seamen, C.H. (1992). Tuckahoe's and Cohees: The Settlers and Cultures of Amherst and Nelson Counties 1607–1807. Virginia: Sweet Briar College Printing Press

Smith, J. C. (1986). Ethnic Genealogy: A Research Guide. Connecticut: Greenwood Press, 1983.

Treaty between Virginia and the Indians 1677. Virginia: The Library of Virginia.

Virginia Colonial Records (1677). Gover'r & Councill of our Colony and Plantacon of Virginia in the West Indys.

Woodson, R. F. & I. (1970). Virginia Tithables, From the Burned Records Counties. Virginia: Isobel B. Woodson.

INDEX

// //

A

Aborigines 129
Africa 37, 57, 97, 153, 162, 173, 182
African 14, 30, 41, 49, 50, 66, 68, 73, 80, 83, 85, 99, 142, 143, 146, 153, 162, 185, 186, 190, 194, 195
African American 1, 4, 7, 45, 49, 50, 59, 60, 77, 79, 166
African American Ancestor 142, 147
African American Community 161
African American Patriots 138
African American President 49, 50
African Americans 3, 11, 36, 50, 60, 84, 177
African Ancestry Lab See Howard University, See Howard University 98
African Cultures 30
African Methodist Episcopal (AME) 17
African Slave 49
African Slaves 80, 83
African-American 60
African-American soldiers See 54th Massachusetts Regiment 59, 166
Airforce 18
Alabama 27
Alaska 83, 186
Alaskan Natives 31
Albany, New York, See Underground Railroad 59

Alexandria Virginia 111, 113, 117
Alexandria, Fredericksburg, and Richmond 84
Virginia 28, 49, 52
Alice (Mulatto) 123
Allele 155
America 11, 13, 14, 44, 50, 53, 54, 64, 65, 83, 99, 129, 130, 170
America's Founding Fathers 50
American Band Stand 6
American Civil War 59, 66, 69, 187
American Colonization Society See Johnson, Elijah 59, 66, 69, 187
American Colonization Society (ACS) 53, 54, 161, 162
American History 27, 28, 49, 199
American Indians 31
American President 49, 50
America's Founders 37, 49
Amherst County 68, 92, 130, 132–138
Amherst County Bond 134, 137
Amherst County household 134, 135, 137, 138
Amherst County Marriage Bond 134, 183
Amherst County Virginia 138
Aminidab See Booker, Aminidab, 91
Amish 44
Amos & Andy 6
Ancestry Chart 151

Ancestry.com 145, 150
Anderson, John 71
Anglican Church 68, 85, 125
Anglican Churches 85
Anglos 99, 163
Anglos and Normans 99
Ann 113, 118, 128, 133, 136, 137
Anti-Slavery, Also See Parker,
    William 61, 64, 68
Antislavery advocates 64
Anti-Slavery Movement 64
Appalachian Chain 26
Appalachian Mountain 23, 26,
    168
Appalachian Mountain Range
    23
Arawak 14
Ash Playground 3
Ashmun Institute See Lincoln
    University 63
Ashmun, Jehudi See Johnson,
    Elijah 53
Asian 50, 142, 146, 164
Asian, African, and European 50
Racial Group 50
A-Tin Lizzie 39
Atlantic Ocean 29
Aunt Betty See Indian Hannah
    24, 25
Aunt Ester 9
Aunt Nanny See Indian
    Hannah 25
Auto Mechanic See Martin,
    Charles 39
Auto Repair Shop 39
Automatic Tie Baler See Ruth,
    Chester 78

B

Baga 76
Guinea West Africa 74, 76
Bahamas 14
Bahamian Dialect See Gullah
    80
Bailey, Obed 52
Baler-feeder See Ruth, Chester
    78
Baptism Record 85
Baptist 22, 67, 68, 92
Baptist Church 22, 67, 68, 92
Baptist Historical Society 67
Baptist Minister 68, 92
Base Pair 155
Basque Region of Spain 99, 155
Batesby, Myles 126
Battersby 127
Battersby, Miles 127
Lancaster County Virginia 84,
    126, 128, 129
Battle of Camden South
    Carolina 109, 110
Battle of Chaffin's Farm
    Virginia 69
Baxter1 1, 4, 7–9, 13, 15–18, 49,
    94, 99, 101, 102, 105, 145, 151
Baxter and Bonaparte,
    Darby, Wright, Boyd, and
    Cheeseborough 17
Baxter, Grandfather See Baxter,
    Charles Wesley 15, 16
Baxter, Alonzo 7
Uncle 4, 7, 9, 38, 62, 63, 65, 66,
    72, 78, 86, 103, 108, 110,
    111, 116, 130
Baxter, Annie 105

Fire-Brand Hill See
Geographical Names of
Chester County First Census
of the United States 115
First Sergeant See Pinn,
Robert A. Fishkill 21
Flat Rock Creek 136
Florida Key 80
Folk Artist 77
Forbes, David See Parker,
William
Ford Automobile 39
Ford Motor Company
Fort Wagner See Tubman,
Harriet
Francis, Joseph (Mulatto) 122
Fredericksburg 67, 68, 84, 85,
90, 91, 92, 95, 111, 122
Virginia 20, 28, 49, 52, 53, 63,
68, 69, 79, 83, 84, 85, 88, 90,
91, 100, 110, 111, 113, 114,
115, 117, 119, 125, 126, 128,
130, 132, 137, 138, 145, 150,
155
Fredericksburg Court Virginia
See 121
Fredericksburg Free Negro
Registry 92
Fredericksburg Registry 119
Fredericksburg Virginia 95, 109
Free Black 26, 54, 62, 121
Free Black Emigrants 54
Free Blacks 51, 63, 64, 84, 92,
116, 126, 143
Free Colored Person (FCP) 37
Free man of color 121, 138
Free Mulatto 91, 115
Free Mulattos 111

Free Negro Registry 91
Fredericksburg Virginia 95, 109
Free Octorara Church 40
Free Patty See Bowden, Patty
Free Persons of Color 6, 111,
120, 139
Free woman of color 121
Freeman, Hannah
Indian Hannah 23, 24
French Creek 20
Fugitive Slave Act 63, 64 Also
See Fugitive Slave Law
Fulani 17, 99
Fulani Tribe 99
Furguson, James 123

G

Galley Page 110
Garland, Mr. 115
Garner, William 127
Geechie 80
Gene 156
Genealogical Research 19, 142,
145, 147, 150
Genealogist 148
General Cornwallis 130
Genome 156
George Washington
Birthplace 89
Georgetown Maryland 62
Georgia 3, 26, 28, 70, 75, 76,
77, 80, 81, 168
Georgia Sea Islands 80
Georgy See Warner, Leah
Germany 155
Gibbons, James 20
Gibbs, James 122
Gilpin, Gideon 25

H

Hague, John 115

Haiti 17

Hall's Regiment See Johnson, Elijah Senior 52

Hanaway, Castner, See Christiana Restisance 60-61, 64

Hannah See Indian Hannah 23–25, 43, 100, 112–114, 123, 134–136

Indian 19–26, 28, 30, 31, 33, 35, 40, 47, 59, 81, 125–130, 143, 158, 162

Hanover County 138

Hanover County Taxpayers 138

Hanway 60

Hanway, Castner, See Parker, William 60–61, 64

Haplogroup (DNA) 13–14, 97–99

Haplogroup K 13

Harding, Warren President 77

Harlan, James 20

Harriet Beecher Stowe 66

Harris 31, 45, 136

Harris, Carolyn 45

Harris, Isham 136

Harrisburg Pennsylvania 46

Hatfield's Cleaners 1

Hay, Charles 115

Hayden, Ezekil 127

Head of Household See Dillion, David 41, 76

Henderson, Daniel and Alexander 22

Henrico County Virginia 111

Henry VIII 99–100

Henry, Samuel (Negro) 122

Henson 38, 62–63, 65–66

Henson, Emory 62

Henson, Josaih 62, 63, 66

Uncle Tom 62, 66

Henson, Josaih and Emory 62

Henson, Josiah 62–63, 66

Henson, Matthew 62

Henson, Thomas J. 38

Hensons 62

Hero of the riot See Parker, William 60

Hezziah See Pinn, Hezziah 127

High-Resolution Match 97–98

Hildruss, Mrs. 115–116

Hillary See Johnson, Hilary R.W. 55

Hilliard, Lydia 86–88, 94–95

Hilton 36, 63, 75, 80

Hilton Head Island 80

Hilton Head South Carolina 75

Hinson, See Hinson Village 62–63

Hinson Village 62

Hinson, Emory 63

Hinson, Josaih 63

Hinsonville 62-63

Hinton, Louise 35

Hispanics 11, 50

As an Ethnic Group 50, 84, 173

Hispaniola 14

Historical Societies 85

History of African-Americans See Parker, William 60

History Sheets 149

Holliday, Billie 16

Hollinger, Barbara 123

Homer, Mr. 91

Indians 14, 19, 20, 22, 23, 24, 28, 29, 31, 33, 34, 37, 38, 44, 45, 46, 50, 58, 59, 84, 125, 126, 145, 158, 159
Indians and blacks 84, 143
Indians in Brazil 50
Indiantown Lancaster County Virginia 84, 126, 128, 129
Insolvency List 121
Internet 73, 145, 150, 152, 153
Iron Ore 3, 85
Iroquoian tribe 34
Iroquois Confederacy 132
Iroquois Confederation 34
Isabella See Warner, Leah
Isaiah and Emma 15
Island Slaves 80
Isolate Communities 28

J

Jacks' Grocery Store 1
Jackson, Also See Booker, Aminidab 91
Jackson, Anne 92, 118
Jackson, Elizabeth 116, 120
Jackson, James 72, 91, 121
Jackson, James and Patty Bowden 91, 116
Jackson, Maria 117, 118, 121
Jackson, Maria and Samuel 92, 116
Jackson, Maria Lewis 91, 116, 117
Jackson, Patty (Martha) Bowden 89, 90, 91, 92
Jackson, Patty and James 91
Jackson, Patty Bowden 89, 90, 91, 92, 93, 116, 118, 121

Jackson, Samuel 91, 92, 116, 118, 120
Jackson, Samuel and Maria Lewis 120
Jackson, Samuel Walter 116, 120
Jackson, Walter 92, 118, 120
Jackson, WalterB. 118
Jacksonian Purges 143
Jacksonville Florida 80
Jacob See Owens, Samuel
Jacob, John and Hiram 121
Nocho 34, 36, 37, 38, 41, 44, 45, 63
Jamaica 14, 80
Jamaican Creole 80
James 20, 35, 52, 71, 72, 85, 86, 88, 91, 93, 114, 115, 116, 119, 121, 122, 125, 128, 129, 133, 138, 139
James Junior, Samuel, William, and Leroy 91
Jackson Children See Jackson, Patty and James 91, 116
James River 115
Jamestown Landing 83
Jamestown Virginia 53
Jamison South Carolina 18
Jefferson, Field 131, 137
Jefferson, Thomas 26
Jemima (Chilton) See Chilton, Thomas 93
Jeremiah, Napoleon, Jin, (or Jinsey), and Perline 15
Jersey Indians See Indian Hannah 24
Jim and William 129

Munro (Monro) See Monroe, William 86, 87, 92
Munro (Monroe) 87
Munro (Monroe), William 88
Munro (Monroe), Wm. 92, 94
Munro(e), William 94
Munroe (Monroe), Jane 93
Munroe (Monroe), William Senior 86, 88
Munroe, Capt., Andrew 88, 93
Munrow, Mary See Monroe, Mary 86, 88, 92
Muslim Religion 76
Muslim Wrap 76
Muslims 76
Mustee, See Underground Railroad 59, 84, 128, 129, 130, 185
Mutation 156

N

Nancy See Lewis, Nancy
Evans 125, 130, 131, 132, 133, 134, 135
Nanticoke 21, 27, 34
Nanticoke River 27
Nanticoke Tribe 27
Nanticoke's 27
Nantmeal 20
Nashville Basin 28
Nat King Cole 6, 8
Nat King Cole show 6
National Census 125
National Geographic Genographics 98, 153
DNA Tests 153
Native 54, 55, 127

Native American 7, 19, 27, 28, 31, 33, 127, 144, 153, 168, 179, 180, 194
Native American Heritage 144
Native Americans, See Underground Railroad 19, 27, 28, 45, 54, 58, 134, 143, 144, 154, 180, 191
Native Ancestors 19, 24
Native Ancestry 36, 73
Native and African Ancestry 73
Native Culture 83
Native of America 130
Native People 19, 83
Natives 23, 36, 85
Natives and Africans 58, 84
Natives and blacks 58, 84, 126
Natives Spiritual Beliefs 30
Negro 53, 83, 91, 158, 159
Negro Fanny 117
Wife of Ambrose Lewis 109, 111, 112, 113, 114, 115, 117, 118, 119
Negro Spiritual 4
Negroes 4, 57, 59, 71, 117, 122, 158, 159
Negroes and Indians See Underground Railroad 59, 159
Nelson County 130
Ness, Elliot 39
New Castle County 24
New England 45
New Jersey 19, 20, 24, 29, 30, 34, 36, 52, 53, 68, 70
New Jersey, Pennsylvania, and Ohio 53

Wright 17, 53
Wright, Rachel See Johnson,
    Elijah 53
Wynard 35, 51

X

xy Chromosomes 98

Y

Y chromosome marker 14
Yarby, Captain 128

Yates See Yates, Charles
Yates, Charles 90, 91, 118
York County VA 138
Yorktown, See The Siege of
    Yorktown 111, 128, 129,
    130

Z

Zachariah See Walker,
    Zachariah 81, 82

ENDNOTES

1. Wills, Anita, Notes and Documents of Free Persons of Color: Four Hundred Years of an African American Family's History, July 2004, Lulu Press:NC
2. Genographic Genetic History: Dr. Anthony Baxter, February 24, 2006
3. The Taino Indians: Native Americans of the Caribbean, http://www.healing-arts.org/spider/tainoindians.htm
4. Strange Fruit, was an anti-lynching poem written by Abe Meeropo,and released as a song on April 20, 1939; performed by Billie Holiday.
5. For more on this see chapter on DNA
6. Strange Fruit, was an anti-lynching poem written by Abe Meeropo,and released as a song on April 20, 1939; performed by Billie Holiday.
7. Excerpt from statement of Leonardo Bellamy Great-Great-Great Grandson of Wynard Bonaparte, October 13, 2008
8. Futhey, J. Smith & Cope, Gilbert, History of Chester County, Pennsylvania With Genealogical and Biographical Sketches; Everts & Co. 1881, Philadelphia:PA
9. Marshall J. Becker, "Hannah Freeman: An Eighteenth-Century Lenape Living and Working Among Colonial Farmers, Pennsylvania Magazine of History and Biography 114 (1990): 251-52
10. History of Berks County, Pennsylvania; http://www.horseshoe.cc/pennadutch/places/pennsylvania/berksco/berks.htm, Sunday August 10, 2003
11. Susquhenna River, March 13, 2009; http://www.greenworks.tv/radio/earthtones/susquehanna.htm
12. History of New Jersey; http://www.aclink.org/HISTORY/mainpages/LENAPE.asp
13. The Green Book, Part II; Narratives and Records to the Present Time, 1888; http://www.unionmills.org/green_book/chapter02.htm

12. Katz, William, L. Black Indians: History's Missing Chapter, American Legacy Magazine Spring 1997; Vol .3/number 1, pg., 38

13. The Green Book, Part II; Narratives and Records to the Present Time, 1888; http://www.unionmills.org/green_book/chapter02.htm

14. Ecenbarger, William, February 9, 1986, The secrets of the Welsh Mountain, The Philadelphia Inquirer Magazine;PA

15. Baxter family history compiled by Anthony Baxter.

16. Burrowe, Carl P., Power and Press Freedom in Liberia, 1830-1970;2005; Africa Press:NJ, pg. 65

17. `The Colony of Liberia, On 11 March 1850; http://www.vahistorical.org/onthisday/31150.htm, Virginia Historical Society

18. Futhey, Smith & Cope, Gilbert;History of Chester county, Pennsylvania with Genealogical and Biographical Sketches; Philadelphia: Louis H. Everts & Co. 1881

19. Lauber, Almon Wheeler; Indian Slavery in Colonial Times Within the Present Limits of the United States, Part I

20. Nineteenth Annual Report of the Bureau of American Ethnology, 1897–1898, p. 233.

21. American Weekly Mercury, October 24, 1734.

22. New York State Library Bulletin, History, No. 4, May, 1900.

23. State of NewWebsite; Underground Railroad, Harriet Tubman; http://www.state.nj.us/nj/about/history/underground_railroad.html

24. Stowe, Harriet Beecher; Uncle Tom's Cabin

25. Gilbert, Jim and Lisa, Chatham Daily News, C-K's black historic sites worth the visit Chatham Canada March 13, 2009, http://chathamdailynews.ca/ArticleDisplay.aspx?e=1424614

26. Pinn, Robert, Wikepedia Free Encyclopedia, March 20, 2009, http://en.wikipedia.org/wiki/Robert_Pinn#Biography

27. Columbia Spy, 21 March 1863, p 2; Lancaster County Historical Society; Lancaster County: PA

28. Indians" of Virginia - The Real First Families of Virginia; http://www.virginiaplaces.org/nativeamerican/index.html (1/5/09)

29. Indians" of Virginia - The Real First Families of Virginia; http://www.virginiaplaces.org/nativeamerican/index.html (1/5/09)

30. Heinegg, Paul; Free African Americans of North Carolina and Virginia; http://www.freeafricanamericans.com/Haws_Hurst.htm

30. Chapmen, John Harper's Weekly, Zach Walker, Sept. 21, 1912, http://www.etymonline.com/cw/zach.htm

31. William And Mary College Quarterly Historical Magazine, (Genealogy of Virginia Families; Vol. III,; Heale-Muscoe, pp. 728–752, 1982).

32. Westmoreland County Virginia Court Orders, 1705–1787, Library of Virginia microfilm reel nos.55-61

33. Westmoreland County Orders 1698–1705, pg., 257; 1705 pg.,21, 22, Westmoreland County Virginia

34. For more information check out The "Atlas of the Human Journey" on the Genographic Project's website:https://www3.nationalgeographic.com/genographic/atlas.html

35. From Lewis Genealogy, http://homepages.rootsweb.ancestry.com/~marshall/esmd45.htm#id626

36. Chapman, John Jay, Harper's Weekly (Sept. 21, 1912); Chapman's book of essays, "Memories and Milestones," (1915)

37. Green, Margaret Givens, email, August 19, 2005

38. Houck, Peter W. & Maxham, Mintcy D,; Indian Island: In Amherst County, Warwick House Publishing, Lynchburg:VA 1993

40. Sutton, K., ibid.

41. Circuit Court Clerk Lancaster County, Virginia, County Court Records, Order Book 9, 1743–1752, p. 160, Lancaster County Courthouse, Lancaster Virginia 22503, Northumberland County Order Book, 1753–56, 213

42. Heinegg, P., Free African Americans of North Carolina And Virginia, (1994), MD: Clearfield Publishing Company; pp.482–483

43. Pinn, John, Revolutionary War Pension Application, 1842, Washington DC :National Archives And Records Administration; File Number R8264

44. ibid, Heinegg, P., Free African Americans of North Carolina And Virginia, (1994), MD: Clearfield Publishing Company; pp.482–483

45. Winkler, Wayne, Walking Toward The Sunset: The Melungeons Of Appalachia, Mercer University Press, 2005, pg. 47

46. Heinegg, Paul; Free African Americans of North Carolina and Virginia; http://freeafricanamericans.com/revolution.htm Historical Society of Delaware; http://www.hsd.org/gengd. htm

47. United States Census Bureau 1989

28293735R00154

Made in the USA
Charleston, SC
07 April 2014